Variations: Three Korean Poets

Variations
사랑의 변주곡
Three Korean Poets

Kim Su-Young
Shin Kyong-Nim
Lee Si-Young

Translated by
Brother Anthony of Taizé
Young-Moo Kim

With love

Anthony

Christmas 2001

East Asia Program
Cornell University
Ithaca, New York 14853

The Cornell East Asia Series is published by the Cornell University East Asia Program (distinct from Cornell University Press). We publish reasonably-priced books on a variety of scholarly topics relating to East Asia as a service to the academic community and the general public. Standing orders, which provide for automatic billing and shipping of each title in the series upon publication, are accepted.

If after review by internal and external readers a manuscript is accepted for publication, it is published on the basis of camera-ready copy provided by the volume author. Each author is thus responsible for any necessary copy-editing and for manuscript formatting. Address submission inquiries to CEAS Editorial Board, East Asia Program, Cornell University, Ithaca, New York 14853-7601.

The translation and publication of this book was supported by the Korean Culture and Arts Foundation and the Korea Literature Translation Institute.

Number 110 in the Cornell East Asia Series
Copyright © 2001 Anthony Teague and Young-Moo Kim. All rights reserved
ISSN 1050-2955
ISBN 1-885445-49-0 hc
ISBN 1-885445-10-5 pb
Library of Congress Control Number: 2001087733
Printed in the United States of America
15 14 13 12 11 10 09 08 07 06 05 04 03 02 01   9 8 7 6 5 4 3 2 1

Cover design by Boram Kim and Karen Smith.

⊗ The paper in this book meets the requirements for permanence of ISO 97061994.

차례   Contents

이 시 영　　Lee Si-Young　199

Introduction

By Jikwan Yoon

This volume invites its readers to assess for themselves the significance of bringing together poems by Kim Su-Young, Shin Kyong-Nim, and Lee Si-Young. The combination of poets and the selection of texts was done by the translators; it reflects the depth of their understanding of modern Korean poetry and its development. Such a volume does not yet exist in Korea, where the three names tend to exist in separate critical spheres. The combination allows us to gain a deeper insight into some of the ways modernity and tradition coexist in contemporary Korean poetry.

The three poets presented here were each born just fourteen years apart, which may in part explain their common poetic spirit and also their ability to confront and probe contemporary issues from the somewhat different viewpoints, which reflect the rapid changes that have occurred within modern Korean history. Each poet expresses the distinct characteristics of a particular time: the 1950s and 60s for Kim Su-Young, the 70s and 80s for Shin Kyong-Nim, and the most recent period for Lee Si-Young, who began his career in the late 1970s and is still active.

They share some things in common linguistically and stylistically, apparently shaped by their involvement in the complex social changes that post-liberation South Korea has faced, and the resulting transformative effects on people's lives. Thus, it is very important to read Korea's sense of longing, its aspiration, and its subconscious in these poems.

A common voice resonates throughout the work of all three poets in the form of a strong moral echo. Dissimilarities appear on the surface: Kim Su-Young echoes the voice of urban sensibility through the complexity and experimentation of his avant-garde verse — contrasting with Shin Kyong-Nim's use of traditional *minjung* language and rhythms that reflect the roots and sentiments of rural farm communities. Lee Si-Young's modernist style and tradi-

xi

tional memory evince a sensibility for and fusion with Kim and Shin, while his linguistic restraint and epigrammatic tropes set him apart. Yet within their very different poems there exists a notion of morality that serves as an essential characteristic of contemporary Korean poetry, prominently manifested under the collective guise of responsibility, duty, self-reflection, and introspection.

A strong moral voice may characterize a nation's poetry and serve as a virtue on its own, but it does not always guarantee nor necessarily accompany poetic accomplishment. In poetry, morality is less the existence of moral articulations than it is a matter of weaving one's voice into poetic grammar and achieving poetic fulfillment. When I observe the moral echo in the work of these three poets, I make a connection between the moral voice found in these poems and their resonance with the notion of conscience that is found throughout contemporary Korean poetry.

The conditions under which depth of conscience becomes the touchstone for a poem's final outcome indicate the specific predicament and prerogative faced by Korean poets. I believe that the challenge and crisis generated by the specific Korean situation is what has created the country's unique contemporary accomplishment in poetry. Their choice of Kim, Shin, and Lee suggests that the translators have recognized and value these poets' quality and sincerity in facing matters of conscience, and in locating those matters as important aspects of contemporary Korean poetry.

The notion of conscience exists in several forms — ethical and emotional, political and social, and intellectual. The type of conscience that appears in poetry is generally not an abstract moral proposition, but is ultimately expressed when the sincerity of a mature poet's temperament unites with emotion and language. In other words, poetic conscience is achieved when temperament and attitude are supported by a penetrating sensibility and emotion and then refined by language.

In this volume, Kim Su-Young's poetic sentiment is steeped in shame and sorrow, Shin Kyong-Nim's in anger and melancholy, and their combined emotional states have been inherited by Lee Si-Young. While these connections are fundamentally lyrical, in this case the lyricism is not the simple baring of one's emotions, but the fusing of lyricism with a sense of the social, that gives their poems conscience. This may be viewed as part of a general contemporary, literary phenomenon in which poetic imagination includes intellectuals' overall societal concerns. However, it is also a distinct characteristic of Third World literature, one which frequently forces intellectuals to honestly confront social and emotional predicaments that have been spotlighted by a forced and hasty modernization process tied to westernization.

The notion of conscience via collective poetic revelation is unavoidably associated with the formation and development of modern Korean poetry, and in a larger sense of modern Korean history. That is, the notion of conscience in contemporary Korean poetry maintains a sense of society which includes the willingness to identify with a great number of oppressed individuals — a willingness which has emerged from the unique manifestations of Korean modernity. This sensibility projects the patriotic tradition of Korean *literati* (i.e., poems depicting honorable integrity, loyalty, and calls for justice) inherited from feudal times, yet is disengaged from this tradition in the poets' attempts to adjust to modernity.

In the sadness that serves as the central sentiment in these poems, one finds a confrontation between the delineation and sublation of tradition and modernity. The distinctive characteristic of Korean poetry has frequently been described as *han* — a problematic description, not only due to the difficulty of defining *han*, but on account of the danger of ideologizing it as a trans-historical feature of Korean literature — an assessment which I find tiresome.

Sadness is one of the most intense of all human sentiments, and we can surely understand its accumulation in the hearts of oppressed people and its tendency to harden into a complex, inconsolable emotion such as resentment. This is also called *han*, but we are not necessarily entitled to use the term 'han literature'. In fact, it is possible in modern times to view colonized victims of extreme persecution as having had *han* superimposed on them. Even though this is the case in Korea, it is incorrect to suggest that *han* is unique and exclusive to this country.

The sadness that flows through the works of these three poets is not simply a sentimental revelation of suppressed emotion, but a fusion with intellect and a sober historical confrontation. In them, the complex emotions buried within the sentiment of sadness combine with the sympathetic memories of our history and undue reliance on *minjung* power; as such, these works should be viewed as historical records of change through language. That a poet can maintain his moral conscience during a time when oppression creates a constant state of crisis confronts him with anguish, resentment, and shame about his life in the present. It is from this that true poetry emanates.

The poetic worlds of Kim, Shin, and Lee grew from their intimate conversations with postcolonial Korea, enriched by the moral and intellectual influences operating within their poetic sensibilities. Thus, a knowledge of Korean society is essential to understanding these poems — i.e., the systematic contradiction arising from the division of the Korean Peninsula and its subsequent Balkanization by the Cold War Powers, coming as it did on the heels of Korea's liberation from Japanese colonialism. The unavoidable outcome was an atrocious civil war, with the two Koreas divided by a cold war ideology which allowed both governments to wield abnormal, distorted power over their respective citizens.

In South Korea's case, it assumed a capitalist framework dependent upon fascist control. Within this structure, South Korea transformed itself into a society in which progressive ideology was constantly situated under severe psychological and physical oppression, conjoined with a suppressed desire and longing for freedom that was both political and moral. These forces shaped the political and literary landscape from the 1950s through the 1980s, during which almost all the poems in this collection were created. It is important to remember that a collective desire for democratization, unification, and independence from oppression penetrates modern Korean literature, resulting in the strong spirit of nationalism and *minjung* that marks Korean poetry.

A primary source of many of Kim Su-Young's poems was the April Revolution of 1960 — both its preconditions and aftermath. While the citizen protagonists of the April Revolution succeeded in toppling a dictatorial government, their dream was immediately thwarted by the military coup d'état that immediately followed. His work occupies an important place in contemporary Korean poetry because of his profound insights into the social dynamics of a society undergoing sudden and rapid change — including the persecution and suppressed desires that social contradictions forced upon pre-revolution intellectuals and the subsequent sense of failure.

Thus, the April Revolution is buried like a political unconscious in Kim's poems. They serve as realistic accounts of the attempt to form an appropriate citizenry for a democratic society, while simultaneously embracing such persistent issues in modern Korean history as the desire for democracy and reunification.

For Kim, the notion of revolution (shown in his occasional substitution of the word 'love' in his poems) is linked to his own hope for a civil society based on compassion, close ties among its citizens, individual freedom, and a sense of unified humanity. On the other side lies his observation of the irony of Korea'stransformation into a society that is frequently bourgeois and philistine. But his satire never falls into self-contempt because it also articulates his strong desire for a civil society.

Comprehensive reevaluations are still being made of Kim's work, in part because his career was cut short by a tragic car accident. The task of assessing Shin Kyong-Nim's and Lee Si-Young's poems is more difficult, since they are still active. This is especially true for Lee, the youngest of the three, whose preference for short, metaphysical poems indicates a potential for further transformation. But it is difficult to deny that Shin has been already placed among the few main voices of contemporary Korean poetry. As Kim Su-Young spoke for the individual citizen, Shin Kyong-Nim speaks for *minjung* — the common people.

He first gained recognition with the 1976 publication of his *Nongmu (Farmers' Dance)* that used *minjung* rhythms with simple, authentic language to record the nation's contemporary trials and tribulations from a farmer's viewpoint. Through his efforts (which cover several decades), Shin has represented the lives of the Korean people and has described both the need for revolutionary change and the latent inherited force found in *minjung* lives. His work also reflects the strength and truth seen in his own life experiences as an intellectual and active participant in various reform movements, which resulted in his serving several prison terms.

Understanding the relationship between *people* and *citizen* is important to understanding Korean society and poetry. At risk of oversimplification, comparing Kim's citizen and Shin's *minjung* leads to the related issue of Korean society's structural complexity in both theoretical and practical terms. The movement to overthrow the military dictatorship since the 1960s grew to be firmly connected to the larger Workers' Movement resulting from the rapid forces of modernization.

Modern society's contradictions were magnified as a large number of peasant farmers relocated to urban centers to work in low-paying, manufacturing jobs. Thus, the 1970s and 1980s witnessed the transformation of this *minjung* underclass into a force behind social change. Shin felt, shared, and spoke for this new force, which eventually effected a transformation towards democracy — the emergence of which Kim Su-Young did not live to see for himself. In Shin's poems we find the embodiment of the liberal ideas that Kim dreamed about, with the energy from an everyday need to live fully bursting into a violent, revolutionary movement. Shin studied the origins of these forces, and made them manifest in linguistic form.

Kim Su-Young's poems articulate Korean modernity through their delineation and reflection of the new urban centers and the lives of their inhabitants. This is not to say that Shin's representation of rural farming communities or his veneration of their inhabitants' spirit is necessarily premodern.

Shin's interest in modern problems is located within the *minjung* movement — geographical, political, and emotional — and his poems confront modern issues through changes effected in the lives of *minjung*. Thus, his representation of traditional *minjung* images and appropriation of traditional *minjung* forms (e.g., *p'an sori*) leads to a confrontation with the *minjung* identity crisis resulting from the rapid modernization and westernization of Korean society.

As in many other Third World countries, this double orientation makes the idea of *minjung* necessary for dealing with Korea's problems of modernity. This raises the question of how to define democracy; within the context just described, we must consider democracy in a sense that goes beyond the general concept of liberal democracy.

The rural farming landscape is significant to the work of both Shin and Lee, but Lee's interest reflects the modern dichotomies and interrelationships between urban and rural Korea — in other words, the typical situation of the 1970s, during which many Koreans left their natal villages to find work in the city, thus living suspended lives between two worlds. Lee's treatment differs from Shin's in terms of a reduced sense of immediacy and familiarity with rural life, making the rural landscape in his poems the object of memories recalled and reflected upon.

In one sense, where Lee has inherited the allure of modern sentiments and the petit bourgeois shackles of city life assessed by Kim, he has also recovered the agrarian memory presented so poignantly and intimately in Shin's poems.

What distinguishes Lee's poetry is his weak attachment to the modernist disposition toward difficulty and incomprehensibility for its own sake. Rather than relying on traditional *minjung* songs, however, Lee uses metaphysical and intellectual language to create more tangible modern images.

In other words, while sympathizing with the traditional, national, *minjung* sentiments originating in and symbolized by real and imaginary rural communities, he also presents a more modern perception of a more modernized reality. This is the attribute that distinguishes Lee not only from his predecessors, but also from the majority of his contemporaries who favor either the modernist or *minjung* approach.

I will end this foreword by emphasizing how the voices of conscience and morality that govern the poems in this collection are connected to the historical consciousness that the three poets clearly possess. The poems' invocations become more vivid when understood within the contexts of the April Revolution (Kim) or the resistance to military dictatorship that marks contemporary Korean history (Shin). Lee's poems reflect his participation in the fight against the same dictatorial regime, but unlike those of his predecessors, they also show the influences of a more developed capitalist system and progressive form of democracy.

Even in Lee's "Tell me, wind," the first poem in his section, the urgency and sincerity of the first three lines (*Tell me, wind, who is in your land? / Are there vast shadows / that come down at sunset and rattle the door latch?*) are diminished considerably if they are read outside the context of the tragic division of North and South, the fates of those partisans and their families who suffered from persecution in the South, and the painful memories of his own parents' experiences as peasant farmers.

In other words, the historicity that colors these poems also strengthens and intensifies their poetic sensibility; in this sense, it is something dissolved into the rich language forms of the poems themselves. Therefore, I would emphasize that overlooking this aspect will result in an inadequate understanding of the poems translated here.

Finally, it is important to recognize the limitations of translation in terms of language, sentiment, and tone — particularly in Shin's poems, which rely on *minjung* rhythms. However, we should also keep in mind that translation is a creative act, and there is no doubt that the work of these respected translators will provide an appropriate introduction to a most important aspect of contemporary Korean poetry.

Jikwan Yoon is a Professor in the Department of English Language and Literature at Duksung Womens' University, Seoul.

Historical Note

For readers unfamiliar with modern Korean history, the following outline may be helpful.

1910: annexation of Korea by Japan.

1945: August 15, surrender of Japan brings liberation to Korea with responsibility for the shift to full independence entrusted jointly to the United States and the USSR, their zones divided by the 38th parallel.

1948: establishment of the Republic of Korea by Syngman Rhee in the south while Kim Il-Sung establishes a communist-style regime in the north.

1950: June 25, attack by the North Korean army across the 38th parallel begins the Korean War. A decision by the United Nations makes this an international conflict.

1953: Armistice agreement creates a demilitarized zone separating the two Koreas.

1960: President Syngman Rhee attempts to change the constitution to allow himself a further term of office. Popular discontent is expressed by demonstrations across the country, involving many high-school and university students. On April 19th the military open fire on these unarmed demonstrators in the streets of Seoul, killed hundreds. Sygman Rhee is forced to stand down.

1961: May 16, General Park Chung-hee stages an "anti-communist" military coup that puts an end to months of liberty during which much debate raged as to the form of democracy best suited to Korea. He promotes a policy of industrialization and modernization.

1972: December 27, President Park Chung-hee proclaims the Yu-shin Constitution which effectively makes him president for life and abolishes all forms of elected representation or political organization. All opposition or criticism is judged subversive. Student demonstrations and other protests become the only means of indicating dissent. Thousands are arrested, tortured and imprisoned in the following years. On October 26, 1979, President Park is assassinated by the head of his security agency. Many hope for a return to civilian-led democracy.

1980: May 18, troops enter Kwangju and suppress peaceful student demonstrations, killing hundreds. General Chun Doo-Hwan declares martial law across the country, thousands of political and intellectual figures are arrested. Chun Doo-Hwan becomes president.

Kim Su-Young
김 수영

Kim Su-Young (Kim Su-Yŏng) was born in Seoul in 1921. He studied for a time in Japan, and in what is now Yonsei University. Some of his early poems were published in 1949 as part of the anthology 새로운 도시와 시민들의 합창 *Seroun tosiwa simindur ŭi hapch'ang* (*The New City and the Chorus of Citizens*). During the Korean war, he was forced to serve in the North Korean army for a time and was subsequently interned on Koje Island until 1952. He later worked as a journalist and also lectured on a part-time basis.

In his lifetime, he only published one volume of poetry, 달나라의 장 난 *Tallara ŭi changnan* (*A Game Played in the Moon*), in 1959. After his death in a car accident in 1968, further collections of poetry and of his critical essays were published. Minumsa Publishing Company published his complete works, poetry and prose, in two volumes (金洙暎 全集 I 詩, II 散文 *Kim Su-Yŏng chŏnchip I shi, II sanmun*) in 1981. The essays 詩여, 침을 뱉어라 *Si yŏ ch'im ŭl pet'ŏra* (*Poetry, spit it out*, 1968) and 反詩論 *Pansiron* (*Theory of Anti-Poetics*, 1968) are particularly important manifestos arguing for a renewal of poetry and aesthetics. While he was deeply influenced by Modernism, his social vision and his growing conviction that poetry should use colloquial language, made him a prophetic pioneer.

1

달나라의 장난

팽이가 돈다
어린아이이고 어른이고 살아가는 것이 신기로워
물끄러미 보고 있기를 좋아하는 나의 너무 큰 눈 앞에서
아이가 팽이를 돌린다
살림을 사는 아이들도 아름답듯이
노는 아이도 아름다워 보인다고 생각하면서
손님으로 온 나는 이집 주인과의 이야기도 잊어버리고
또한번 팽이를 돌려주었으면 하고 원하는 것이다
도회(都會)안에서 쫓겨다니는 듯이 사는
나의 일이며
어느 소설보다도 신기로운 나의 생활이며
모두 다 내던지고
점잖이 않은 나의 나이와 나이가 준 나의 무게를 생각하면서
정말 속임없는 눈으로
지금 팽이가 도는 것을 본다
그러면 팽이가 까맣게 변하여 서서 있는 것이다
누구 집을 가보아도 나 사는 곳보다는 여유(餘裕)가 있고
바쁘지도 않으니
마치 별세계(別世界)같이 보인다
팽이가 돈다
팽이가 돈다
팽이 밑바닥에 끈을 돌려 매이니 이상하고
손가락 사이에 끈을 한끝 잡고 방바닥에 내어던지니
소리없이 회색빛으로 도는 것이
오래 보지 못한 달나라의 장난같다
팽이가 돈다
팽이가 돌면서 나를 울린다
제트기 벽화밑의 나보다 더 뚱뚱한 주인 앞에서

Games in the Land of the Moon

A top is spinning.
Life enthralls me, child's or adult's;
I love to watch, I gaze open-eyed
as a child spins a top.
How beautiful a child at play is;
children playing at housekeeping are really beautiful.
I forget to converse with the man I am here to visit,
longing for the child to spin the top again.
Casting everything aside, even my work,
(I live in the city as one pursued
and my life
is more enthralling than any novel)
conscious of my age and the dignity age brings,
here I am, solemnly sitting,
watching with candid eyes a top spinning.
The top turns black as it spins.
Every house I visit is more relaxed,
        less frantic than mine,
quite out of this world, in fact.
The top is spinning.
The top is spinning.
A string wound round the foot of the top, most strange,
one end between the fingers,
the top thrown to the floor,
and there it spins, soundless, pale gray,
a game played in the moon, long unseen down here.
The top is spinning.
The spinning top moves me to tears.

나는 결코 울어야 할 사람은 아니며
영원히 나 자신을 고쳐가야 할 운명과 사명에 놓여있는 이 밤에
나는 한사코 방심조차 하여서는 아니될 터인데
팽이는 나를 비웃는 듯이 돌고 있다
비행기 프로펠러보다는 팽이가 기억이 멀고
강한 것보다는 약한 것이 더 많은 나의 착한 마음이기에
팽이는 지금 수천년전의 성인과같이
내 앞에서 돈다
생각하면 서러운 것인데
너도 나도 스스로 도는 힘을 위하여
공통된 그 무엇을 위하여 울어서는 아니된다는 듯이
서서 돌고 있는 것인가
팽이가 돈다
팽이가 돈다

I mustn't cry before the man of the house, he's stouter than me,
below the plane painted on his wall;
this evening is assigned to my destiny, my mission
to be forever improving myself;
it would not do for me to be the least bit inattentive,
yet the top spins on and on, as if mocking me.
Tops lie farther back in my memory than propellers,
more weak things than strong make up my kind heart,
and the top is spinning before me now
like a sage from a past millennium.
It's a sad thing, come to think of it,
but as it spins upright it seems to be saying:
"We must not weep, you and I, for our power to spin,
since that is something we both share."
The top is spinning.
The top is spinning.

(1953)

구라중화 (九羅重花)

— 어느 소녀에게 물어보니
너의 이름은 글라지오라스라고

저것이야말로 꽃이 아닐 것이다
저것이야말로 물도 아닐 것이다

눈에 걸리는 마지막 물건이 무엇이냐고 물어보는 듯
영롱한 꽃송이는 나의 마지막 인내를 부숴버리려고 한다

나의 마음을 딛고 가는 거룩한 발자국소리를 들으면서
지금 나는 마지막 붓을 든다

누가 무엇이라 하든 나의 붓은 이 시대를 진지하게 걸어가는
사람에게는 치욕

물소리 빗소리 바람소리 하나 들리지 않는 곳에
나란히 옆으로 가로 세로 위로 아래로 놓여있는
무수한 꽃송이와 그 그림자
그것을 그리려고 하는 나의 붓은 말할수없이 깊은 치욕

이것은 누구에게도 보이지 않을 글이기에
(아아 그러한 시대가 온다면 얼마나 좋은 일이냐)
나의 동요없는 마음으로
너를 다시한번 치어다보고 혹은 내려다보면서
무량의 환희에 젖는다

꽃 꽃 꽃
부끄러움을 모르는 꽃들
누구의 것도 아닌 꽃들

A Gladiolus

— When asked, the girl replied:
Your name is Gladiolus.

No, that will never be a flower.
No, that will never be water, either.

A gaudy flower is attacking my last reserves of patience,
asking what was the very last object caught by my eye.

Still hearing the sacred footsteps that trampled on my heart
as they went their way, I take up my pen one last time.

No matter what anyone says, my pen brings disgrace to people
on their solemn passage through this age.

In a place where there is no sound of water, rain, or wind,
countless flowers, with their shadows, stand in rows,
sideways, crossways, upwards, downwards;
my pen, eager to depict them all, brings utter deep disgrace.

This is writing that no one will see.
(How wonderful if such an age were to come.)
Looking up and down at you all
with an untroubled heart
I experience immense delight.

Flowers, flowers, flowers,
flowers quite ignorant of shame,
flowers belonging to no one,

너는 늬가 먹고 사는 물의 것도 아니며
나의것도 아니고 누구의 것도 아니기에
지금 마음놓고 고즈너기 날개를 펴라
마음대로 뛰놀 수 있는 마당은 아닐지나
(그것은 골고다의 언덕이 아닌
현대의 가시철망 옆에 피어있는 꽃이기에)
물도 아니며 꽃도 아닌 꽃일지나
너의 숨어있는 인내와 용기를 다하여 날개를 펴라

물이 아닌 꽃
물같이 엷은 날개를 펴며
너의 무게를 안고 날아가려는 듯

늬가 끊을 수 있는 것은 오직 생사의 선조(線條)뿐
그러나 그 비애에 찬 선조(線條)도 하나가 아니기에
너는 다시 부끄러움과 주저(躊躇)를 품고 숨가뻐하는가

결합된 색깔은 모두가 엷은 것이지만
설움이 힘찬 미소와 더불어 관용과 자비로 통하는 곳에서
네가 사는 엷은 세계는 자유로운 것이기에
생기와 신중을 한몸에 지니고

사실은 벌써 결하여있을 너의 꽃잎 우에
이중의 봉오리를 맺고 날개를 펴고
죽음 우에 죽음 우에 죽음을 거듭하리
구라중화

not belonging to the water you live by,
not mine, no one's:
freely spread your quiet wings.
This is no garden where you can frolic contentedly
(these flowers bloom beside today's barbed-wire fences,
not on Golgotha)
and you are flowers which are neither water nor flowers.
Deploy your hidden patience and valor, spread your wings.

Flowers that are not water,
spreading wings thin as water,
as if about to fly off bearing all your weight;

all that can put an end to anyone is the fine thread between
life and death, yet that filament full of grief is not single.
Is that why you are gasping, harboring shame and vacillation?

All your colors combined are thin, yet
where sorrow is known as forbearance and mercy,
with a sorrowful smile, the thin world you inhabit is free;
so, cherishing vigor and prudence entirely,

fixing two buds spread like wings
above your already doomed petals,
you repeat death above death above death:
gladiolus.

(1954)

도취(陶醉)의 피안

내가 사는 지붕 우를 흘러가는 날짐승들이
울고가는 울음소리에도
나는 취하지 않으련다

사람이야 말할수없이 애처로운 것이지만
내가 부끄러운 것은 사람보다도
저 날짐승이라 할까
내가 있는 방 우에 와서 앉거나
또는 그의 그림자가 혹시나 떨어질까보아 두려워하는 것도
나는 아무것에도 취하여 살기를 싫어하기 때문이다

하루에 한번씩 찾아오는
수치와 고민의 순간을 너에게 보이거나
들키거나 하기가 싫어서가 아니라

나의 얇은 지붕 우에서 솔개미같은
사나운 놈이 약한 날짐승들이 오기를 노리면서 기다리고
더운 날과 추운 날을 가리지 않고
늙은 버섯처럼 숨어있기 때문에도 아니다

날짐승의 가는 발가락 사이에라도 잠겨있을 운명 —
그것이 사람의 발자욱소리보다도
나에게 시간을 가르쳐주는 것이 나는 싫다

나야 늙어가는 몸 우에 하잘것없이 앉아있으면 그만이고
너는 날아가면 그만이지만
잠시라도 나는 취하는 것이 싫다는 말이다

Paradise of Rapture

I refuse to go into raptures
over the songs of the feathered creatures
that pass singing above the roof where I live.

We humans are unspeakably pathetic, true, but still,
am I supposed to say that those flying creatures
provoke more shame than humans do?
They may come and perch just above me in my room,
I tremble to think that their shadows might vanish
for I hate living in raptures about anything.

Yet it's not because I hate to be seen, discovered
at moments of disgrace and anguish
as they come on their visit once a day;

not because fierce sparrow-hawks are lurking
like ancient mushrooms up on my frail roof;
on hot days and cold without distinction, they wait
with glaring eyes for helpless, feathered creatures to come.

I hate the way destiny, lodged
between those birds' thin claws,
teaches me the passing of time
more than any human footsteps can.

I do not mind if you perch there, wretched, as I grow old,
I do not mind if you fly away;
but I really hate being in raptures, even for a moment.

나의 초라한 검은 지붕에
너의 날개소리를 남기지 말고
네가 던지는 조그마한 그림자가 무서워
벌벌 떨고 있는
나의 귀에다 너의 엷은 울음소리를 남기지 말아라

차라리 앉아있는 기계와같이
취하지 않고 늙어가는
나와 나의 겨울을 한층더 무거운 것으로 만들기 위하여
나의 눈이랑 한층 더 맑게 하여다우
짐승이여 짐승이여 날짐승이여
도취의 피안에서 날아온 무수한 날짐승이여

Don't leave the sound of your wings
on my shabby black roof.
Don't leave your faint chirping in my ear
as I shudder
in fear of the tiny shadows you cast.

Only make my eyes clearer, like some engine perched there
to make me and my winter even heavier,
as I remain without rapture and grow ever older.
Creatures, creatures, feathered creatures,
innumerable, feathered creatures
from the Paradise of Rapture.

(1954)

나의 가족

고색이 창연한 우리집에도
어느덧 물결과 바람이
신선한 기운을 가지고 쏟아져들어왔다

이렇게 많은 식구들이
아침이면 눈을 부비고 나가서
저녁에 들어올 때마다
먼지처럼 인색하게 묻혀가지고 들어온 것

얼마나 장구(長久)한 세월이 흘러갔던가
파도처럼 옆으로 혹은 세대를 가리키는 지층의 단면처럼
억세고도 아름다운 색깔 —

누구 한 사람의 입김이 아니라
모든 가족의 입김이 합치어진 것
그것은 저 넓은 문창호의 수많은
틈 사이로 흘러들어오는 겨울바람보다도 나의 눈을 밝게 한다

조용하고 늠름한 불빛 아래
가족들이 저마다 떠드는 소리도
귀에 거슬리지 않는 것은
내가 그들에게 전령을 맡긴 탓인가
내가 지금 순한 고개를 숙이고
온 마음을 다하여 즐기고 있는 서책은
위대한 고대조각의 사진(寫眞)

그렇지만
구차한 나의 머리에

My Family

In no time at all, waves and winds
have burst into our antiquated house,
bringing fresh vigor with them.

The many people in my family
go out in the morning, rubbing their eyes,
then return home with it in the evening; every day,
they return meanly covered with it like a kind of dust.

I wonder how long it has been.
Sideways, like waves, or like a section of strata
suggestive of generations, unyielding and lovely of hue . . .

Not the breath of any one person
but the whole family's breath combining
makes my eyes shine brighter than the winter winds
flowing through the gaps of our wide windows and doors.

In the quiet, solemn lamplight,
the sound of each member of the family in uproar
does not offend the ear,
perhaps because I have entrusted my whole spirit to them.
Now I bow my docile head
and wholeheartedly enjoy a book
of photos of great classical sculptures.

Still, the momentary impulses
filling my poor head

성스러운 향수와 우주의 위대함을
담아주는 삽시간의 자극을
나의 가족들의 기미많은 얼굴에
비(比)하여 보아서는 아니될 것이다

제각각 자기 생각에 빠져있으면서
그래도 조금이나 부자연한 곳이 없는
이 가족의 조화와 통일을
나는 무엇이라고 불러야 할 것이냐

차라리 위대한 것을 바라지 말았으면
유순한 가족들이 모여서
죄없는 말을 주고받는
좁아도 좋고 넓어도 좋은 방안에서
나의 위대의 소재를 생각하고 더듬어보고 짚어보지 않았으면

거칠기 짝이없는 우리집안의
한없이 순하고 아득한 바람과 물결 ─
이것이 사랑이냐
낡아도 좋은 것은 사랑뿐이냐

with sacred yearnings and cosmic greatness
cannot bear comparison
with my family's faces
and their countless freckles.

;

I wonder what I should call
the harmony and unity of this family,
each one plunged deep in private thoughts
yet totally devoid of unnaturalness.

I hope I do not expect anything very great,
just the docile family together, exchanging innocent talk
in a room that may be small or spacious, no matter;
I hope I will not try to reflect on, examine, scrutinize
the whereabouts of my greatness.

The infinitely pure, distant wind and waves
of our incomparably rough-cast folk . . .
Is this love?
Are things old yet good the all of love?

(1954)

여름 아침

여름아침의 시골은 가족과 같다
햇살을 모자같이 이고 앉은 사람들이 밭을 고르고
우리집에도 어저께는 무씨를 뿌렸다
원활(圓滑)하게 굽은 산등성이를 바라보며
나는 지금 간밤의 쓰디쓴 후각과 청각과 미각과 통각마저
잊어버리려고 한다

물을 뜨러 나온 아내의 얼굴은
어느틈에 저렇게 검어졌는지 모르나
차차 시골동리사람들의 얼굴을 닮아간다
뜨거워질 햇살이 산 위를 걸어내려온다
가장 아름다운 이기적인 시간 우에서
나는 나의 검게 타야 할 정신을 생각하며
구별을 용서하지 않는
밭고랑 사이를 무겁게 걸어간다

고뇌여
강물은 도도하게 흘러내려가는데
천국도 지옥도 너무나 가까운 곳

사람들이여
차라리 숙련(熟練)이 없는 영혼이 되어
씨를 뿌리고 밭을 갈고 가래질을 하고 고물개질을 하자

여름아침에는
자비로운 하늘이 무수한 우리들의 사진을 찍으리라
단 한장의 사진을 찍으리라

A Summer Morning

The countryside on a summer's morning is like a family.
Wearing hats of sunshine, people squat working the fields.
Yesterday our folk sowed radish seed.
Gazing up at the smoothly crouching mountain ridges
I try to forget last night's bitter sense
of smell, hearing, taste, of perception, even.

The face of my wife, emerging to draw water,
has grown very dark; when did that happen?
It's getting just like the faces of the village folk.
Sunlight that will soon grow scorching comes marching
over the hills. In this loveliest selfish hour
I ponder on my soon-to-be-sunburned mind
as I plod heavily between furrows
unforgiving of all discrimination.

Ah, agony.
The river goes rushing powerfully onward
while heaven and hell are very near.

Ah, these people.
We must turn into souls unskilled
and sow seed, plow fields, dig, delve, and rake.

This summer morning
the loving heavens will surely snap our countless forms,
snap just a single snapshot.

(1956)

눈

눈은 살아있다
떨어진 눈은 살아있다
마당 위에 떨어진 눈은 살아있다

기침을 하자
젊은 시인이여 기침을 하자
눈 위에 대고 기침을 하자
눈더러 보라고 마음놓고 마음놓고
기침을 하자

눈은 살아있다
죽음을 잊어버린 영혼과 육체를 위하여
눈은 새벽이 지나도록 살아있다

기침을 하자
젊은 시인이여 기침을 하자
눈을 바라보며
밤새도록 고인 가슴의 가래라도
마음껏 뱉자

Snow

The snow is alive.
The fallen snow is alive.
The snow that has fallen in the yard is alive.

Let's have a cough.
Young poet, let's have a cough.
Let's have a cough aimed at the snow.
Make the snow look up, then freely, freely,
let's have a cough.

The snow is alive.
For soul and body oblivious of death
the snow is alive as the morning breaks.

Let's have a cough.
Young poet, let's have a cough.
Looking out at the snow,
let's have a spit:
all the phlegm accumulated in your lungs overnight.

(1956)

폭포

폭포는 곧은 절벽을 무서운 기색도 없이 떨어진다

규정할 수 없는 물결이
무엇을 향하여 떨어진다는 의미도 없이
계절과 주야를 가리지 않고
고매한 정신처럼 쉴사이없이 떨어진다

금잔화도 인가도 보이지 않는 밤이 되면
폭포는 곧은 소리를 내며 떨어진다

곧은 소리는 소리이다
곧은 소리는 곧은
소리를 부른다

번개와같이 떨어지는 물방울은
취(醉)할 순간조차 마음에 주지 않고
나타(懶惰)와 안정을 뒤집어놓은 듯이
높이도 폭(幅)도 없이
떨어진다

A Waterfall

The waterfall drops over the lofty cliff with no sign of fear.

The uncontrollable spate drops
with no sense of falling toward anything,
making no distinction between night and day,
like a noble mind, never pausing for rest.

When nightfall comes, ox-eye and houses hid from sight,
the waterfall drops with upright sound.

The upright sound is its sound.
Upright sound calls out
to upright sound.

The water drops, falling like lightning,
drops
without height or breadth
as if confounding sloth and rest,
not granting the mind a moment's rapture.

(1957)

봄밤

애타도록 마음에 서둘지 말라
강물 위에 떨어진 불빛처럼
적적한 업적을 바라지 말라
개가 울고 종이 들리고 달이 떠도
너는 조금도 당황하지 말라
술에서 깨어난 무거운 몸이여
오오 봄이여

한없이 풀어지는 피곤한 마음에도
너는 결코 서둘지 말라
너의 꿈이 달의 행로와 비슷한 회전을 하더라도
개가 울고 종이 들리고
기적소리가 과연 슬프다 하더라도
너는 결코 서둘지 말라
서둘지 말라 나의 빛이여
오오 인생이여

재앙과 불행과 격투와 청춘과 천만인의 생활과
그러한 모든것이 보이는 밤
눈을 뜨지 않은 땅속의 벌레같이
아둔하고 가난한 마음은 서둘지 말라
애타도록 마음에 서둘지 말라
절제여
나의 귀여운 아들이여
오오 나의 영감(靈感)이여

Springtime Evening

Never hasten to be anxious in your heart.
Do not aspire to achievements as dazzling
as light falling on a stream.
Dogs may bark, bells may echo, the moon may rise,
never let yourself be flustered.
Heavy body, awakening from drink:
oh, springtime.

Even with a heart infinitely faint from fatigue,
never hasten.
Your dreams may soar like the moon on its way,
dogs may bark, bells echo,
whistles may wail their sad laments,
you must never hasten.
Do not hasten, my light.
Oh, human life.

On an evening when every kind of thing can be seen:
misfortune, misery, fighting, youth, the lives of millions,
like insects unseeing beneath the ground,
do not let your dull poverty-stricken heart hasten.
Never hasten to be anxious in your heart.
Ah, moderation,
my darling son,.
Oh, my inspiration.

(1957)

채소밭 가에서

기운을 주라 더 기운을 주라
강바람은 소리도 고웁다
기운을 주라 더 기운을 주라
달리아가 움직이지 않게
기운을 주라 더 기운을 주라
무성하는 채소밭가에서
기운을 주라 더 기운을 주라
돌아오는 채소밭가에서
기운을 주라 더 기운을 주라
바람이 너를 마시기 전에

Beside a Vegetable Patch

Give strength, more strength.
How lovely, the sound of river breezes.
Give strength, more strength.
To keep the dahlias from moving,
give strength, more strength.
At the side of this exuberant vegetable patch,
give strength, more strength.
At the side of this returning vegetable patch,
give strength, more strength.
Before the breeze drinks you up.

(1957)

서시

나는 너무나 많은 첨단의 노래만을 불러왔다
나는 정지의 미에 너무나 등한하였다
나무여 영혼이여
가벼운 참새같이 나는 잠시 너의
흉하지 않은 가지 위에 피곤한 몸을 앉힌다
성장은 소크라테스 이후의 모든 현인들이 하여온 일
정리는
전란에 시달린 이십세기 시인들이 하여놓은 일
그래도 나무는 자라고 있다 영혼은
그리고 교훈은 명령은
나는
아직도 명령의 과잉을 용서할 수 없는 시대이지만
이 시대는 아직도 명령의 과잉을 요구하는 밤이다
나는 그러한 밤에는 부엉이의 노래를 부를 줄도 안다

지지한 노래를
더러운 노래를 생기없는 노래를
아아 하나의 명령을

Prologue

I have been singing too many avant-garde songs.
I have been too neglectful of the beauty of stillness.
Trees! Soul!
For a moment, I will perch my weary body,
light as a sparrow, on your not so unseemly branches.
Maturing has been the task of every sage since Socrates,
putting in order
is the task of poets in this strife-ridden twentieth century.
Still the trees grow on; the soul, too, and precepts, commands.
While I belong
to a generation unable to forgive excessive commands,
though this generation is a night that demands
    excessive commands.
I know how to sing like an owl in a night such as this.

A wretched song,
a filthy song, a lifeless song:
ah, yet another command.

(1957)

초봄의 뜰안에

초봄의 뜰안에 들어오면
서편으로 난 난간문 밖의 풍경은
모름지기
보이지 않고

황폐한 강변을
영혼보다도 더 새로운 해빙의 파편(破片)이
저멀리
흐른다

보석같은 아내와 아들은
화롯불을 피워가며 병아리를 기르고
짓이긴 파냄새가 술취한
내 이마에 신약처럼 생긋하다

흐린 하늘에 이는 바람은
어제가 다르고 오늘이 다른데
옷을 벗어놓은 나의 정신은
낡은 바위에 앉은 이끼처럼 추워라

겨울이 지나간 밭고랑 사이에 남은
고독은 신의 무재조(無才操)와 사기라고
하여도 좋았다

A Yard in Early Springtime

If you enter the yard in early springtime,
you cannot see
the landscape outside the westward gate
as it should be seen.

Far off in the distance,
even fresher than souls, thawing fragments of ice
go drifting
down the sides of the river.

My wife and son, precious as jewels,
are raising chickens, feeding a brazier,
while the odor of pulped leeks like some miracle remedy
gently strokes my drunken brow.

In the cloudy sky the rising wind
differs today from yesterday's
and my mind, stripped naked,
is cold as the moss on ancient rocks.

You may well call the solitude
left where winter has passed among the furrows
divine incompetence or imposture.

(1958)

비

비가 오고 있다
여보
움직이는 비애(悲哀)를 알고 있느냐

명령하고 결의하고
「평범(平凡)하게 되려는 일」 가운데에
해초(海草)처럼 움직이는
바람에 나부껴서 밤을 모르고
언제나 새벽만을 향하고 있는
투명(透明)한 움직임의 비애(悲哀)를 알고 있느냐
여보
움직이는 비애(悲哀)를 알고 있느냐

순간이 순간을 죽이는 것이 현대
현대가 현대를 죽이는 「종교(宗敎)」
현대의 종교는 「출발」에서 죽는 영예
그 누구의 시처럼

　　그러나 여보
　　비오는 날의 마음의 그림자를
　　사랑하라
　　너의 벽에 비치는 너의 머리를
　　사랑하라
비가 오고 있다
움직이는 비애여

결의하는 비애
변혁하는 비애……

Rain

Rain is falling.
Say,
are you acquainted with moving sorrow?

Command, resolve:
in the midst of "trying to be ordinary"
are you acquainted with the sorrow of transparent motion
streaming in the wind
that moves like seaweed, ignoring night,
ever only advancing dawnward?
Say:
are you acquainted with moving sorrow?

Moment killing moment is today.
Today is "religion" killing today.
Today's religion is honor dying at the start
like someone's poem.

Yet, I say,
you should love
the shadow of a rainy day's heart.
You should love
your head reflected on your wall.
Rain is falling.
Moving sorrow!

Resolving sorrow
reforming sorrow . . .

현대의 자살
그러나 오늘은 비가 너 대신 움직이고 있다
무수한 너의 「宗敎」를 보라

계사(鷄舍) 위에 울리는 곡괭이소리
동물의 교향곡(交響曲)
잠을 자면서 머리를 식히는 사색가(思索家)
―모든 곳에 너무나 많은 움직임이 있다

여보
비는 움직임을 제하는 결의
움직이는 휴식

여보
그래도 무엇인가가 보이지 않느냐
그래서 비가 오고 있는데!

Present-day suicide,
yet today rain is moving in your stead.
Consider all your countless "religions."

A sound of hoes ringing above the henhouse,
the animals' symphony,
a thinker cooling his head as he sleeps
— there is too much motion everywhere.

I say:
rain is the resolve controlling motion,
repose in motion.

I say:
can you still not see anything?
That's why rain is falling.

(1958)

밤

부정한 마음아

밤이 밤의 창을 때리는구나

너는 이런 밤을 무수한 거부 속에 헛되이 보냈구나

또 지금 헛되이 보내고 있구나

하늘아래 비치는 별이 아깝구나

사랑이여

무된 밤에는 무된 사람을 축복하자

Night

Unclean heart!

Why, night is beating at night's windows.

You have wasted this night in countless refusals.

You are wasting it now, too.

How pitiful the stars that shine here below.

Love!

In this night made void let us bless those made void.

(1958)

모리배(謀利輩)

언어는 나의 가슴에 있다
나는 모리배들한테서
언어의 단련을 받는다
그들은 나의 팔을 지배하고 나의
밥을 지배하고 나의 욕심을 지배한다

그래서 나는 우둔한 그들을 사랑한다
나는 그들을 생각하면서 하이덱거를
읽고 또 그들을 사랑한다
생활과 언어가 이렇게까지 나에게
밀접해진 일은 없다

언어는 원래가 유치한 것이다
나도 그렇게 유치하게 되었다
그러니까 내가 그들을 사랑하지 않을 수가 없다
아아 모리배여 모리배여
나의 화신이여

A Profiteer

There's language in my breast.
I receive language-training
from profiteers.
They control my arms, control
my food, control my desires.

So I love those thickheads.
With them in mind, I read
Heidegger and love them still.
I have never before known life and language
were so closely connected.

Language is basically a childish thing.
I have become equally childish,
which is why I cannot help but love them.
Ah, profiteer from profiteers,
my other self.

(1959)

생활(生活)

시장거리의 먼지나는 길옆의
좌판 위에 쌓인 호콩 마마콩 멍석의
호콩 마마콩이 어쩌면 저렇게 많은지
나는 저절로 웃음이 터져나왔다

모든것을 제압(制壓)하는 생활 속의
애정처럼
솟아오른 놈

(유년의 기적(奇蹟)을 잃어버리고
얼마나 많은 세월(歲月)이 흘러갔나)

여편네와 아들놈을 데리고
낙오자(落伍者)처럼 걸어가면서
나는 자꾸 허허 — 웃는다

무위와 생활의 극점(極點)을 돌아서
나는 또하나의 생활의 좁은 골목 속으로
들어서면서
이 골목이라고 생각하고 무릎을 친다

생활은 고절(孤絶)이며
비애(悲哀)이었다
그처럼 나는 조용히 미쳐간다
조용히 조용히 . . . .

Life

I burst out laughing
on seeing just how many peanuts and mamanuts
were spread on the layers of matting prepared for them
on planks along the dusty alleys of the market.

A rascal bursting out
like love
in a life where everything is tightly controlled .

(How many ages have passed,
the wonders of infancy all forgotten?)

So I go walking on, like some outcast,
with wife and sonny-boy there beside me
as I keep laughing on and on: Ha ha . . .

Passing around inaction and the high point of life,
then penetrating
into another of life's narrow alleys,
I think: this is an alley, full of glee.

Life has been loneliness
and sorrow.
I am quietly going mad,
quietly, very quietly . . .

(April 30, 1959)

달밤

언제부터인지 잠을 빨리 자는 습관이 생겼다
밤거리를 방황할 필요가 없고
착잡한 머리에 책을 집어들 필요가 없고
마지막으로 몽상을 거듭하기도 피곤해진 밤에는
시골에 사는 나는 ―
달밝은 밤을
언제부터인지 잠을 빨리 자는 습관이 생겼다

이제 꿈을 다시 꿀 필요가 없게 되었나보다
나는 커단 서른아홉살의 중턱에 서서
서슴지않고 꿈을 버린다

피로를 알게 되는 것은 과연 슬픈 일이다
밤이여 밤이여 피로한 밤이여

Moonlit Night

I've recently made a habit of sleeping early —
no need to wander through night-time streets,
no need to pick up a book for a muddled mind,
since I live in the country and at last,
when I'm exhausted with constant daydreaming,
I've recently made a habit of sleeping early
on bright moonlit nights.

It's as if I don't need to dream any more.
Standing at the great midpoint, my thirty-ninth year,
I have resolutely given up dreaming.

To know weariness is a sorrowful thing.
Night, night, weary night!

(May 22, 1959)

사령(死靈)

— 활자(活字)는 반짝거리면서 하늘아래에서
간간이
자유를 말하는데
나의 혼은 죽어있는 것이 아니냐

벗이여
그대의 말을 고개숙이고 듣는 것이
그대는 마음에 들지 않겠지
마음에 들지 않어라

모두다 마음에 들지 않어라
이 황혼(黃昏)도 저 돌벽아래 잡초(雜草)도
담장의 푸른 페인트빛도
저 고요함도 이 고요함도

그대의 정의도 우리들의 섬세(纖細)도
행동(行動)이 죽음에서 나오는
이 욕된 교외(郊外)에서는
어제도 오늘도 내일도 마음에 들지 않어라

그대는 반짝거리면서 하늘아래에서
간간이
자유를 말하는데
우스워라 나의 영(靈)은 죽어있는 것이 아니냐

A Ghost

. . . The letters sparkling here below
speak of freedom from time to time,
yet my soul seems dead.

Old friend,
you surely cannot be pleased
that I am listening to you with meekly bowed head.
It should not please you.

Nothing at all is pleasing:
this twilight, the weeds at the foot of that stone wall,
the color of the green paint on the fence,
that stillness, this stillness,

your righteousness, our delicacy,
and in this disgraceful suburb
where action arises from death —
yesterday, today, tomorrow, nothing is pleasing.

Sparkling here below,
you speak of freedom from time to time
and yet,
how odd, my soul seems dead.

(1959)

하⋯⋯그림자가 없다

우리들의 적은 늠름하지 않다
우리들의 적은 카크 다글라스나 리챠드 위드마크 모양으로
사나웁지도 않다
그들은 조금도 사나운 악한(惡漢)이 아니다
그들은 선량(善良)하기까지도 하다
그들은 민주주의자를 가장(假裝)하고
자기들이 양민(良民)이라고도 하고
자기들이 선량(選良)이라고도 하고
자기들이 회사원(會社員)이라고도 하고
전차(電車)를 타고 자동차(自動車)를 타고
요리(料理)집엘 들어가고
술을 마시고 웃고 잡담(雜談)하고
동정(同情)하고 진지(眞摯)한 얼굴을 하고
바쁘다고 서두르면서 일도 하고
원고도 쓰고 치부도 하고
시골에도 있고 해변가에도 있고
서울에도 있고 산보도 하고
영화관에도 가고
애교도 있다
그들은 말하자면 우리들의 곁에 있다

우리들의 전선(戰線)은 눈에 보이지 않는다
그것이 우리들의 싸움을 이다지도 어려운 것으로 만든다
우리들의 전선은 당게르크도 놀만디도 연희고지도 아니다
우리들의 전선은 지도책 속에는 없다
그것은 우리들의 집안 안인 경우도 있고
우리들의 직장인 경우도 있고
우리들의 동리인 경우도 있지만⋯

Ha . . . No Shadows

Our enemies are nothing to look at.
Our enemies do not look fierce
like Kirk Douglas or Richard Widmark.
They are not at all fierce villains.
They are even virtuous.
They disguise themselves as democrats.
They term themselves good citizens.
They term themselves the People's Choice.
They term themselves company employees.
They ride in trams, they ride in cars,
they go into restaurants,
they drink, they laugh, they gossip,
their faces express sympathy, sincerity,
they do their work quickly, say they're busy,
write texts, keep accounts,
they're in the countryside, by the seaside,
in Seoul, they take walks,
go to movies,
have charm.
Which means to say that they're right beside us.

Our battle line is invisible to the eye.
Which makes our combat all that more difficult.
Our battle line is not at Dunkirk, or Normandy, or Yonhui Hill.
Our battle line cannot be found in any atlas.
Sometimes it lies in our homes.
Sometimes it lies in our work-places.
Sometimes it lies in our neighborhoods but

보이지는 않는다

우리들의 싸움의 모습은 초토작전이나
「건 힐의 혈투(血鬪)」모양으로 활발하지도 않고
보기좋은 것도 아니다
그러나 우리들은 언제나 싸우고 있다
아침에도 낮에도 밤에도 밥을 먹을 때에도
거리를 걸을 때도 환담(歡談)을 할 때도
장사를 할 때도 토목공사를 할 때도
여행을 할 때도 울 때도 웃을 때도
풋나물을 먹을 때도
시장에 가서 비린 생선냄새를 맡을 때도
배가 부를 때도 목이 마를 때도
연애를 할 때도 졸음이 올 때도 꿈속에서도
깨어나서도 또 깨어나서도 또 깨어나서도…
수업을 할 때도 퇴근시(退勤時)에도
싸이렌소리에 시계를 맞출 때도 구두를 닦을 때도…
우리들의 싸움은 쉬지 않는다

우리들의 싸움은 하늘과 땅 사이에 가득차있다
민주주의의 싸움이니까 싸우는 방법도
민주주의식으로 싸워야 한다
하늘에 그림자가 없듯이 민주주의의 싸움에도 그림자가 없다
하… 그림자가 없다

하… 그렇다…
하… 그렇지…
아암 그렇구 말구…… 그렇지 그래……

응응…… 응…… 뭐?
아 그래…… 그래 그래.

it is invisible.

In appearance our combat follows no burnt-earth strategy
or "Battle at Gun Hill," neither is it nice to see.
Yet we are all the time fighting.
Morning, noon, and night, as we eat,
as we walk down the street, as we enjoy a chat,
as we do business, as we engage in engineering works,
as we go on journeys, as we weep and as we laugh,
as we eat spring greens,
as we go to the market and sniff the smell of fish,
fully fed, and thirsty,
making love, dozing off, in dreams,
waking up, and waking up, and waking up . . .
as we sit in class, as we go home
as we set our watches to the siren,
as our shoes are shined . . .
our combat knows no rest.

Our combat fills all the space between heaven and earth.
It's democracy's battle, so it has to be fought democratically.
As there are no shadows in the heavens, likewise
democracy's battles know no shadows.
    Ha . . . no shadows.

    Ha . . . just so . . .
    Ha . . . and yet . . .
    Why, just so indeed . . . that's how it is . . . .

    Uhuh . . . uh . . . what?
    Ah, I see . . . I see, I see.

                                        (April 3, 1960)

우선 그놈의 사진을 떼어서 밑씻개로 하자

우선 그놈의 사진을 떼어서 밑씻개로 하자
그 지긋지긋한 놈의 사진을 떼어서
조용히 개굴창에 넣고
썩어진 어제와 결별하자
그놈의 동상이 선 곳에는
민주주의의 첫 기둥을 세우고
쓰러진 성스러운 학생들의 웅장한
기념탑을 세우자
아아 어서어서 썩어빠진 어제와 결별하자

이제야말로 아무 두려움 없이
그놈의 사진을 태워도 좋다
협잡과 아부와 무수한 악독의 상징인
지긋지긋한 그놈의 미소하는 사진을 —
대한민국의 방방곡곡에 안 붙은 곳이 없는
그놈의 점잖은 얼굴의 사진을
동회란 동회에서 시청이란 시청에서
회사란 회사에서
XX단체에서 00협회에서
하물며는 술집에서 음식점에서 양화점에서
무역상에서 개솔린 스탠드에서
책방에서 학교에서 전국의 국민학교란 국민학교에서 유치원에서
선량한 백성들이 하늘같이 모시고
아침저녁으로 우러러보던 그 사진은
사실은 억압과 폭정의 방패이었느니
썩은놈의 사진이었느니
아아 살인자의 사진이었느니

First Tear Down His Photo

First tear down his photo and use it to wipe your arse.
Tear down that dreadful fellow's photo,
quietly lay it in the sewer
and let's take our leave of rotten yesterday.
In the spot where that fellow's statue stood
let's raise up democracy's first pillar,
let's raise up a splendid memorial
to our sacred fallen student martyrs.
Ah, quick, let's take our leave of rotten yesterday.

Now there's nothing to be afraid of,
it's all right to set fire to his photo:
the smiling photo of that dreadful fellow,
the very symbol of fraud, of sycophancy, every kind of vice . . .
stuck up in every last nook and cranny of the land,
the photo of that fellow's so genteel face:
in neighborhood offices and city halls,
in every company office,
in this and that meeting place, and association hall,
to say nothing of bars, diners, shoe shops,
trading offices, gasoline stalls,
bookstores, schools, every primary school in the land,
and in nursery schools;
everywhere honest citizens venerated it,
gazing up at that photo morning and night.
It was truly the shield of oppression and tyranny
the photo of a rotten fellow,
and ah, the photo of a murderer . . .

너도 나도 누나도 언니도 어머니도
철수도 용식이도 미스터 강도 류중사도
강중령도 그놈의 속을 모르는 바는 아니었지만
무서워서 편리해서 살기 위해서
빨갱이라고 할까보아 무서워서
돈을 벌기 위해서는 편리해서
가련한 목숨을 이어가기 위해서
신주처럼 모셔놓던 의젓한 얼굴의
그놈의 속을 창자밑까지도 다 알고는 있었으나
타성같이 습관같이
그저그저 쉬쉬하면서
할말도 다 못하고
기진맥진해서
그저그저 걸어만 두었던
흉악한 그놈의 사진을
오늘은 서슴지않고 떼어놓아야 할 날이다

밑씻개로 하자
이번에는 우리가 의젓하게 그놈의 사진을 밑씻개로 하자
허허 웃으면서 밑씻개로 하자
껄껄 웃으면서 구공탄을 피우는 불쏘시개라도 하자
강아지장에 깐 짚이 젖었거든
그놈의 사진을 깔아주기로 하자 ─

민주주의는 인제는 상식으로 되었다
자유는 이제는 상식으로 되었다
아무도 나무랄 사람은 없다
아무도 붙들어갈 사람은 없다

군대란 군대에서 장학사의 집에서
관공사의 집에서 경찰의 집에서
민주주의를 찾은 나라의 군대의 위병실에서

You and I and sisters and brothers and mothers,
Ch'ol-su and Yong-sik, Mister Kang, Sergeant Yu
and Lieutenant Colonel Kang,
we all knew what the fellow was really like
but put up with it, afraid, playing safe in order to live,
afraid of being dubbed a Red,
finding it useful, in order to earn,
in order to continue our miserable lives,
we venerated that dignified face like our ancestor's shrine
though we all knew that fellow to the deep of his guts
but from sheer inertia, from force of habit,
always on the hush-hush, not able to say all we wanted to say,
utterly worn out and exhausted,
we would always keep hanging up
that wicked fellow's photo
and today's the day it must be firmly torn down.

Let's use it to wipe our arses with.
Let's gravely use the fellow's photo to wipe our arses with.
Laughing merrily, let's use it to wipe our arses.
Laughing gaily, let's use it to kindle our coal briquettes.
The straw's all wet in the puppy's kennel?
Let's spread the fellow's photo there instead . . .

Democracy's become a matter of common sense.
Freedom's become a matter of common sense.
Nobody's going to scold us.
Nobody's going to arrest us.

From army barracks, from school inspectors' houses,
from the homes of public officials and policemen,
from army guard-rooms, from the rooms of division

사단장실에서 정훈감실에서
민주주의를 찾은 나라의 교육가들의 사무실에서
사·일구후의 경찰서에서 파출소에서
민중의 벗인 파출소에서
협잡을 하지 않고 뇌물을 받지 않는
관공사의 집에서
역이란 역에서
아아 그놈의 사진을 떼어 없애야 한다

우선 가까운 곳에서부터
차례차례로
다소곳이
조용하게
미소를 띄우면서

영숙아 기환아 천석아 준이야 만용아
프레지덴트 김 미스 리
정순이 박군 정식이
그놈의 사진일랑 소리없이 떼어 치우고

우선 가까운 곳에서부터
차례차례로
다소곳이
조용하게
미소를 띄우면서
극악무도한 소름이 더덕더덕 끼치는
그놈의 사진일랑 소리없이
떼어 치우고 ―

commanders, of chief information officers,
in this land that has found democracy,
from the offices of teachers in this land
      that has found democracy,
from police stations and police boxes after April 19,
from police boxes now friendly to the simple folk,
from the homes of public officials no longer engaged in fraud,
no longer accepting bribes, and from every railway station,
that fellow's photo must be torn down and destroyed.

First from the places close at hand
in proper order, one by one,
ever so gently
quietly now
smiling away

Yong-suk, Ki-hwan, Ch'on-suk, Chun-yi, Man-yong,
President Kim, Miss Lee,
Chong-sun, young Park, Chong-sik,
silently tear down and destroy that fellow's photo,

first from places close at hand
in proper order, one by one,
ever so gently
quietly now
smiling away
silently tear down and destroy that fellow's photo
so wicked, inhuman, it makes you shudder . . .

                                    (At dawn, April 26, 1960)

기도(祈禱)

시를 쓰는 마음으로
꽃을 꺾는 마음으로
자는 아이의 고운 숨소리를 듣는 마음으로
죽은 옛 연인을 찾는 마음으로
잊어버린 길을 다시 찾은 반가운 마음으로
우리가 찾은 혁명을 마지막까지 이룩하자

물이 흘러가는 달이 솟아나는
평범한 대자연의 법칙을 본받아
어리석을만치 소박하게 성취한
우리들의 혁명을
배암에게 쐐기에게 쥐에게 삵괭이에게
진드기에게 악어에게 표범에게 승냥이에게
늑대에게 고슴도치에게 여우에게 수리에게 빈대에게
다치지 않고 깎이지 않고 물리지 않고 더럽히지 않게

그러나 쟝글보다도 더 험하고
소용돌이보다도 더 어지럽고 해저보다도 더 깊게
아직까지도 부패와 부정과 살인자와 강도가 남아있는 사회
이 심연(深淵)이나 사막이나 산악보다도
더 어려운 사회를 넘어서

이번에는 우리가 배암이 되고 쐐기가 되더라도
이번에는 우리가 쥐가 되고 삵괭이가 되고 진드기가 되더라도
이번에는 우리가 악어가 되고 표범이 되고 승냥이가 되고
늑대가 되더라도
이번에는 우리가 고슴도치가 되고 여우가 되고 수리가 되고

A Prayer

A song for the students who died for the nation on April 19, 1960

With the heart of one writing a poem,
with the heart of one picking flowers,
with the heart of one hearing the breath of a sleeping babe.
with the heart of one seeking a sweetheart who died,
with the glad heart of one who lost his way then found it again,
let's see our newly found revolution through to the end.

Imitating the common laws of nature
by which water flows and moons rise,
since achieving our revolution
was simple to the point of folly,
we must keep it from being hurt, slashed, diverted, soiled
by snake, by caterpillar, rat, or lynx,
by mite, by crocodile, panther, coyote,
by wolf, by hedgehog, fox, eagle, or bug,

then passing beyond this society,
far more perilous than the jungle,
more dizzying than a maelstrom, deeper than the ocean,
society still has its corruptions, injustices, murderers, thieves,
harder to cross than abyss or desert or mountain range

though now we may turn into snakes, into caterpillars,
though now we may turn into rats, or lynx, or mites,
though now we may turn into crocodiles, panthers,
coyotes, or wolves,
though now we may turn into hedgehogs or foxes,

빈대가 되더라도
아아 슬프게도 슬프게도 이번에는
우리가 혁명이 성취하는 마지막날에는
그런 사나운 추잡한 놈이 되고 말더라도

나의 죄있는 몸의 억천만개의 털구멍에
죄라는 죄가 가시같이 박히어도
그야 솜털만치도 아프지는 않으려니

시를 쓰는 마음으로
꽃을 꺾는 마음으로
자는 아이의 고운 숨소리를 듣는 마음으로
죽은 옛 연인을 찾는 마음으로
잊어버린 길을 다시 찾은 반가운 마음으로
우리는 우리가 찾은 혁명을 마지막까지 이룩하자

into eagles or bugs,
though we may turn into such dread, filthy creatures,
ah sadly, sadly, now, on that final day
when our revolution is achieved,

though all my sins be hammered home like thorns
into the trillion pores of my sin-filled body,
still not a single hair of mine will be hurt, so

with the heart of one writing a poem,
with the heart of one picking flowers,
the heart of one hearing the quiet breath of a sleeping babe,
with the heart of one seeking a sweetheart who died,
with the glad heart of one who lost his way then found it again,
let's see our newly found revolution through to the end.

(May 18, 1960)

푸른 하늘을

푸른 하늘을 제압하는
노고지리가 자유로왔다고
부러워하던
어느 시인의 말은 수정되어야 한다

자유를 위해서
비상하여 본 일이 있는
사람이면 알지
노고지리가
무엇을 보고
노래하는가를
어째서 자유에는
피의 냄새가 섞여있는가를
혁명은
왜 고독한 것인가를

혁명은
왜 고독해야 하는 것인가를

The Blue Sky

Jealous,
a poet once said that the skylark was free
as it mastered the blue sky;
but that must be modified.

Those who have soared aloft
for the sake of freedom
know
what it is
the skylark sees
that makes it sing;
they know why the smell of blood
must mingle with freedom,
why revolution
is a lonely thing

why revolution
is bound to be a lonely thing.

(June 15, 1960)

가다오 나가다오

이유는 없다 —
나가다오 너희들 다 나가다오
너희들 미국인과 소련인은 하루바삐 나가다오
말갛게 행주질한 비어홀의 카운터에
돈을 거둬들인 카운터 위에
적막이 오듯이
혁명이 끝나고 또 시작되고
혁명이 끝나고 또 시작되는 것은
돈을 내면 또 거둬들이고
돈을 내면 또 거둬들이고 돈을 내면
또 거둬들이는
석양에 비쳐 눈부신 카운터같기도 한 것이니

이유는 없다 —
가다오 너희들의 고장으로 소박하게 가다오
너희들 미국인과 소련인은 하루바삐 가다오
미국인과 소련인은 「나가다오」와 「가다오」의 차이가 있을뿐
말갛게 개인 글 모르는 백성들의 마음에는
「미국인」과 「소련인」도 똑같은 놈들
가다오 가다오
「4월혁명」이 끝나고 또 시작되고
끝나고 또 시작되고 끝나고 또 시작되는 것은
잿님이할아버지가 상추씨, 아욱씨, 근대씨를 뿌린 다음에
호박씨, 배추씨, 무씨를 또 뿌리고
호박씨, 배추씨를 뿌린 다음에
시금치씨, 파씨를 또 뿌리는
석양에 비쳐 눈부신
일년 열두달 쉬는 법이 없는

Be Off with You, Away with You

There is no special reason . . .
Just get out, all of you, go on, get out.
Americans, Soviets, get out, don't delay.
Just as loneliness descends
on a cleanly wiped beer-hall counter,
the counter where money is taken,
so too revolution ends and begins,
and revolution beginning and ending
is like a counter shining bright in the sunset,
money paid and taken,
money paid and taken, paid
and taken.

There is no special reason . . .
Go away, go back to your homes, quite simply go away.
Americans, Soviets, go away, don't delay.
Americans, Soviets: go away, get out, the only difference
between you two is that between "go away" and "get out."
In our people's hearts, unable to write, transparent of speech,
Americans and Soviets are all the same.
Go away, go away.
The way our "April Revolution" ends and begins,
ends and begins, ends and begins
is like wild riverside fields
where Sooty's grandpa first sows lettuce seed, mallow seed,
chard seed, then pumpkin seed, cabbage seed, turnip seed,
then after pumpkin and cabbage sows spinach seed, leek seed,
twelve months a year shining bright in the sunset,

걸찍한 강변밭같기도 할 것이니

지금 참외와 수박을
지나치게 풍년이 들어
오이, 호박의 손자며느리값도 안되게
헐값으로 넘겨버려 울화가 치받쳐서
고요해진 명수할버이의
잿물거리는 눈이
비둘기 울음소리를 듣고 있을 동안에
나쁜 말은 안하니
가다오 가다오

지금 명수할버이가 명석 위에 넘어져 자고 있는 동안에
가다오 가다오
명수할버이
잿님이할아버지
경복이할아버지
두붓집할아버지는
너희들이 피지도를 침략했을 당시에는
그의 아버지들은 아직 젖도 떨어지기 전이었다니까
명수할버이가 불쌍하지 않으냐
잿님이할아버지가 불쌍하지 않으냐
두붓집할아버지가 불쌍하지 않으냐
가다오 가다오

선잠이 들어서
그가 모르는 동안에
조용히 가다오 나가다오
서푼어치값도 안되는 미·소인은
초콜렛, 커피, 페치코오트, 군복, 수류탄
따발총....을 가지고
적막이 오듯이

with not a moment's rest.

Now here we are in a year with a big glut
of melons and water-melons,
they fetch no better price than baby cucumbers and pumpkins,
they go for a song yet Cleary's grandpa
with his weepy eye,
quiet with pent-up anger,
says never a bad word
as he listens to the pigeons cooing,
so go away, go away.

Now, while Cleary's grandpa is asleep, sprawled on a mat,
go away, go away.
Cleary's grandpa,
Sooty's grandpa,
Boony's grandpa,
the old man at the *tubu* stall
At the time you occupied Fiji Island
their fathers were still at their mothers' breasts.
Don't you feel sorry for Cleary's grandpa?
Don't you feel sorry for Sooty's grandpa?
Don't you feel sorry for the old man at the *tubu* store?
Go away, go away.

While they're dozing there,
all unawares,
go away quietly, go on, get out.
Americans, Soviets, not worth a farthing.
Take your chocolate, coffee, petticoats, uniforms,
hand grenades, your automatic rifles,
and as solitude comes,

적막이 오듯이
소리없이 가다오 나가다오
다녀오는 사람처럼 아주 가다오!

solitude comes,
silently go away, get out.
Like departing visitors, go away, for good!

(August 4, 1960)

그 방을 생각하며

혁명은 안되고 나는 방만 바꾸어버렸다
그 방의 벽에는 싸우라 싸우라 싸우라는 말이
헛소리처럼 아직도 어둠을 지키고 있을 것이다

나는 모든 노래를 그 방에 함께 남기고 왔을 게다
그렇듯 이제 나의 가슴은 이유없이 메말랐다
그 방의 벽은 나의 가슴이고 나의 사지일까
일하라 일하라 일하라는 말이
헛소리처럼 아직도 나의 가슴을 울리고 있지만
나는 그 노래도 그 전의 노래도 함께 다 잊어버리고 말았다

혁명은 안되고 나는 방만 바꾸어버렸다
나는 인제 녹슬은 펜과 뼈와 광기(狂氣) ―
실망의 가벼움을 재산으로 삼을 줄 안다
이 가벼움 혹시나 역사일지도 모르는
이 가벼움을 나는 나의 재산으로 삼았다

혁명은 안되고 나는 방만 바꾸었지만
나의 입속에는 달콤한 의지의 잔재 대신에
다시 쓰디쓴 냄새만 되살아났지만

방을 잃고 낙서를 잃고 기대를 잃고
노래를 잃고 가벼움마저 잃어도

이제 나는 무엇인지 모르게 기쁘고
나의 가슴은 이유없이 풍성하다

Remembering That Room

The revolution has failed, I've only moved to another room.
The "Fight, Fight, Fight," on the walls of the previous room
may still be there in the dark — vain words.

I left every song behind in that room when I moved out.
So now for no clear reason my heart is dry,
as if the walls of that room were my heart and limbs.
The words "Work, Work, Work,"
are still ringing, in vain, in my heart but
I have quite forgotten all the songs, those former songs, too.

The revolution has failed, I've only moved to another room.
I am skilled at finding my wealth in despair's lightness:
rusty pens, bare bones, madness.
Maybe this lightness is history too,
and I've made that lightness my wealth.

The revolution has failed, I've only moved to another room.
In my mouth, in place of sweet remnants of will,
I find nothing but a bitter savor come alive again

yet though I lose room, and words, and expectations,
lose songs, and even lightness,

I do not know why, but I am glad;
for no reason, my heart is overflowing.

(October 30, 1960)

사랑

어둠 속에서도 불빛 속에서도 변치않는
사랑을 배웠다 너로해서

그러나 너의 얼굴은
어둠에서 불빛으로 넘어가는
그 찰나에 꺼졌다 살아났다
너의 얼굴은 그만큼 불안하다

번개처럼
번개처럼
금이 간 너의 얼굴은

Love

Because of you I learned love
unchanging in darkness as in firelight

yet as your face
passing from darkness to firelight,
for a moment vanished and reappeared,
your face seems just that much anxious.

Your face, forked
like lightning
like lightning.

(1961)

檄文

新歸去來　2

마지막의 몸부림도
마지막의 양복도
마지막의 신경질도
마직막의 다방도
기나긴 골목길의 순례도
「어깨」도
허세도
방대한
방대한
방대한
모조품도
막대한
막대한
막대한
막대한
모방도
아아 그리고 저 도봉산보다도
더 큰 증오도
굴욕도
계집애 종아리에만
눈이 가던 치기도
그밖의 무수한 잡동사니 잡념까지도
깨끗이 버리고
깨끗이 버리고
깨끗이 버리고
깨끗이 버리고

Public Exhortation

A new homecoming after resigning office 2

One final struggle and
one final suit and
one last show of nerves and
one last coffee shop and
the pilgrimage up the lengthy alley and
a hooligan and
a bluff and
an enormous
enormous
enormous
sham and
a colossal
colossal
colossal
colossal
imitation and
that hatred rising higher
than Dobong Mountain and
disgrace and
the childishness that
used only to eye girls' legs and
countless other miscellaneous distractions
cleanly set aside
cleanly set aside
cleanly set aside
cleanly set aside
cleanly set aside

깨끗이 버리고
깨끗이 버리고
깨끗이 버리고
농부의 몸차림으로 갈아입고
석경을 보니
땅이 편편하고
집이 편편하고
하늘이 편편하고
물이 편편하고
앉아도 편편하고
서도 편편하고
누워도 편편하고
도회와 시골이 편편하고
시골과 도회가 편편하고
신문이 편편하고
시원하고
뼈쓰가 편편하고
시원하고
하수도가 편편하고
시원하고
뽐프의 물이 시원하게 쏟아져나온다고
어머니가 감탄하니 과연 시원하고
무엇보다도
내가 정말 시인이 됐으니 시원하고
인제 정말
진짜 시인이 될 수 있으니 시원하고
시원하다고 말하지 않아도 되니
이건 진짜 시원하고
이 시원함은 진짜이고
자유다

cleanly set aside
cleanly set aside
changing into farming clothes
then looking at the evening scenery
the ground is all right
the house is all right
the sky is all right
the water is all right
sitting down is all right
standing up is all right
lying down is all right
town and country are all right
country and town are all right
the newspaper is all right
and cool
the bus is all right
and cool
the sewers are all right
and cool
as mother admires
the water flows from the pump, it really is cool
above all
I have really become a poet, I feel cool
at last, really,
I can become a real poet, I feel cool
I do not even have to say I feel cool
it really is cool
this coolness is real
it's freedom.

(June 12, 1961)

누이야 장하고나!
新歸去來 7

누이야
풍자가 아니면 해탈이다
너는 이 말의 뜻을 아느냐
너의 방에 걸어놓은 오빠의 사진
나에게는 「동생의 사진」을 보고도
나는 몇번이고 그의 진혼가를 피해왔다
그전에 돌아간 아버지의 진혼가가 우스꽝스러웠던것을 생각하고
그래서 나는 그 사진을 십년만에 곰곰이 정시(正視)하면서
이내 거북해서 너의 방을 뛰쳐나오고 말았다
십년이란 한 사람이 준 상처를 다스리기에는 너무나 짧은 세월이다

누이야
풍자가 아니면 해탈이다
네가 그렇고
내가 그렇고
네가 아니면 내가 그렇다
우스운 것이 사람의 죽음이다
우스워하지 않고서 생각할 수 없는 것이 사람의 죽음이다
팔월의 하늘은 높다
높다는 것도 이렇게 웃음을 자아낸다

누이야
나는 분명히 그의 앞에 절을 했노라
그의 앞에 엎드렸노라
모르는 것 앞에는 엎드리는 것이
모르는 것 앞에는 무조건하고 숭배하는 것이
나의 습관이니까

You're Marvelous, Sister!
A new homecoming after resigning office 7

Sister,
it's either satire or nirvana.
Do you know what that means?
I've seen your big brother's photo hanging in your room,
for me it's the photo of my little brother,
yet I've several times shunned his memorial rites.
I used to consider the memorial rites for father,
who died before him, rather ridiculous
and as a result it's been ten years since I last examined
that photo closely
and I felt so awkward, I rushed straight out of your room.
Ten years is too short a period to master the wounds
one person has inflicted.

Sister,
it's either satire or nirvana.
It's so for you
it's so for me
it's so for you or me.
A person's death is an amusing thing.
A person's death is always unthinkable, unless it's amusing.
The August sky is high and clear.
High, clear things provoke the same amusement.

Sister,
frankly, I fell to my knees before him.
I fell prostrate before him.

동생뿐이 아니라
그의 죽음뿐이 아니라
혹은 그의 실종뿐이 아니라
그를 생각하는
그를 생각할 수 있는
너까지도 다 함께 숭배하고 마는 것이
숭배할 줄 아는 것이
나의 인내이니까

「누이야 장하고나!」
나는 쾌활한 마음으로 말할 수 있다
이 광대한 여름날의 착잡한 숲속에
홀로 서서
나는 돌풍(突風)처럼 너한테 말할 수 있다
모든 산봉우리를 걸쳐온 돌풍처럼
당돌하고 시원하게
도회에서 달아나온 나는 말할 수 있다
「누이야 장하고나!」

Because I usually
fall prostrate before things I don't know,
venerate unconditionally things I don't know.
Not only my little brother.
Not only his death.
Not only his disappearance.
Because it is my fortitude
to venerate together all those who think of him,
all those who can think of him, including you.

"You're marvelous, sister!"
I can speak with a cheery heart.
Standing alone
in this tangled wood on this vast summer day
I can speak to you like a gust of wind.
Like a gust of wind that has passed over every peak,
rash and cool,
fresh from the city, I can say:
"You're marvelous, sister!"

(August 5, 1961)

먼 곳에서부터

먼 곳에서부터
먼 곳으로
다시 몸이 아프다

조용한 봄에서부터
조용한 봄으로
다시 내 몸이 아프다

여자에게서부터
여자에게로

능금꽃으로부터
능금꽃으로……

나도 모르는 사이에
내 몸이 아프다

From Somewhere Far Away

From somewhere far away
to somewhere far away
the body aches again.

From quiet springtime
to quiet springtime
my body aches again.

From woman
to woman

from crab-apple blossom
to crab-apple blossom . . .

unknowingly
my body aches.

(September 30, 1961)

백지에서부터

하얀 종이가 옥색으로 노란 하드롱지가
이 세상에는 없는 빛으로 변할만큼 밝다
시간이 나비모양으로 이 줄에서 저 줄로
춤을 추고
그 사이로
사월의 햇빛이 떨어졌다
이런때면 매년 이맘때쯤 듣는
병아리 우는 소리와
그의 원수인 쥐소리를 혼동한다

어깨를 아프게 하는 것은
노후의 미덕은 시간이 아니다
내가 나를 잊어버리기 때문에
개울과 개울 사이에
하얀 모래를 골라 비둘기가 내려앉듯
시간이 내려앉는다

머리를 아프게 하는 것은
두통의 미덕은 시간이 아니다
내가 나를 잊어버리기 때문에
바다와 바다 사이에
지금의 사월의 구름이 내려앉듯
진실이 내려앉는다

하얀 종이가 분홍으로 분홍 하늘이
녹색으로 또 다른 색으로 변할만큼 밝다
―그러나 혼색은 흑색이라는 걸 경고해준 것은
소학교 때 선생님……

From a White Sheet of Paper

It is so bright that white paper turns jade, brown paper
turns a color unknown in this world.
Time goes dancing
from one line to the next like a butterfly
and in between
April sunlight is falling.
At this same time every year we mistake
the chirping of chicks
for the sound of rats, their enemies.

It is not time that is the virtue of old age,
that makes the shoulders ache.
Because I forget myself
time drops down and settles
as a dove drops down and settles, choosing the white sand
between stream and stream.

It is not time that is the virtue of headaches,
that makes the head ache.
Because I forget myself
truth drops down and settles
as these March clouds drop down and settle
between sea and sea.

It is so bright that white paper turns pink, and pink turns
the azure of the sky if not some other color.
— Only there was a teacher in primary school
who warned us that blended colors are always black . . .

후란넬 저고리

낮잠을 자고나서 들어보면
후란넬 저고리도 훨씬 무거워졌다
거지의 누더기가 될락말락한
저놈은 어제 비를 맞았다
저놈은 나의 노동의 상징
호주머니 속의 소눈깔만한 호주머니에 들은
물뿌리와 담배부스러기의 오랜 친근
윗호주머니나 혹은 속호주머니에 들은
치부책노릇을 하는 종이쪽
그러나 돈은 없다
— 돈이 없다는 것도 오랜 친근이다
— 그리고 그 무게는 돈이 없는 무게이기도 하다
또 무엇이 있나 나의 호주머니에는?
연필쪽!
옛날 추억이 들은 그러나 일년내내 한번도 펴본 일이 없는
죽은 기억의 휴지
아무것도 집어넣어본 일이 없는 왼쪽 안호주머니
— 여기에는 혹시 휴식의 갈망이 들어있는지도 모른다
— 휴식의 갈망도 나의 오랜 친근한 친구이다……

A Flannel Jacket

When I pick up my flannel jacket
after a daytime nap, it feels a lot heavier.
That little fellow, a floppy mess more like a beggar's rags
got soaked in yesterday's rain.
That little fellow is the emblem of my labor:
the long familiarity of cigarette holder and tobacco shreds
in the cows-eye-sized pouch in my pocket,
the slip of paper in my top pocket or inner pocket
that serves as my account-book
but there is no money.
— Having no money is a matter of long familiarity too.
— Of course, this weight is the weight of having no money.
What else is there in my pockets? A pencil!
A scrap of paper with dead memories,
where memories once were noted
but that was never unfolded for a whole year after that.
The left-hand inner pocket has never had anything in it.
— Perhaps it contains a hope of rest?
— Hope of rest is my long familiar friend too . . .

(April 29, 1963)

85

거대한 뿌리

나는 아직도 앉는 법을 모른다
어쩌다 셋이서 술을 마신다 둘은 한 발을 무릎 위에 얹고
도사리지 않는다 나는 어느새 남쪽식으로
도사리고 앉았다 그럴때는 이 둘은 반드시
以北친구들이기 때문에 나는 나의 앉음새를 고친다
팔·일오 후에 김병욱이란 시인은 두 발을 뒤로 꼬고
언제나 일본여자처럼 앉아서 변론을 일삼았지만
그는 일본대학에 다니면서 사년동안을 제철회사에서
노동을 한 강자다

나는 이사벨 버드 비숍여사와 연애하고 있다 그녀는
1893년에 조선을 처음 방문한 영국왕립지학협회회장이다
그녀는 인경전의 종소리가 울리면 장안의
남자들이 모조리 사라지고 갑자기 부녀자의 세계로
화하는 극적인 서울을 보았다 이 아름다운 시간에는
남자로서 거리를 무단통행할 수 있는 것은 교군꾼,
내시, 외국인의 종놈, 관사들 뿐이었다 그리고
심야에는 여자는 사라지고 남자가 다시 오입을 하러
활보하고 나선다고 이런 기이한 관습을 가진 나라를
세계 다른곳에서는 본 일이 없다고
천하를 호령한 민비는 한번도 장안외출을 하지 못했다고……

전통은 아무리 더러운 전통이라도 좋다 나는 광화문
네거리에서 시구문의 진창을 연상하고 인환(寅煥)네
처갓집 옆의 지금은 매립한 개울에서 아낙네들이
양잿물 솥에 불을 지피며 빨래하던 시절을 생각하고
이 우울한 시대를 패러다이스처럼 생각한다

Colossal Roots

I still do not know how to sit properly.
Three of us were having a drink. Two were sitting
with one foot resting on top of the knee, not cross-legged,
while I was sitting in southern style, simply cross-legged.
On such occasions, the other two being from the northern parts,
I adjust my sitting position. After Liberation in '45, one poet,
Kim Pyong-wook, used to sit like a Japanese woman,
kneeling as he talked. He was tough; he spent four years
working in an iron company, attending university in Japan.

I am in love with Isabel Bird Bishop. She was the first head
of the Royal Geographical Society to visit Korea, in 1893.
She saw the dramatic scene as Seoul abruptly changed
into a world of women, men vanishing as a curfew gong rang.
A beautiful time: only bearers, eunuchs, foreigners' servants,
and government officials were allowed to walk the streets.
Then she described how at midnight the women disappeared,
the men emerged, swaggering off to their debaucheries.
She had not seen any country with such a remarkable custom
anywhere else in the world, she said, while Queen Min,
who ruled the country, could never leave her palace . . .

Traditions, no matter how filthy, are good. I pass
Kwanghwamun, recall the mud there used to be by the wall,
remember how women heated cauldrons of lye
and did their washing by In-hwan's hut in the stream bed,
filled in now, seeing those grim times as a kind of Paradise.

버드 비숍여사를 안 뒤부터는 썩어빠진 대한민국이
괴롭지 않다 오히려 황송하다 역사는 아무리
더러운 역사라도 좋다
진창은 아무리 더러운 진창이라도 좋다
나에게 놋주발보다도 더 쨍쨍 울리는 추억이
있는 한 인간은 영원하고 사랑도 그렇다

비숍여사와 연애를 하고 있는 동안에는 진보주의자와
사회주의자는 네에미 씹이다 통일도 중립도 개좆이다
은밀도 심오도 학구도 체면도 인습도 치안국
으로 가라 동양척식회사, 일본 영사관, 대한민국관사,
아이스크림은 미국놈 좆대강이나 빨아라 그러나
요강, 망건, 장죽, 종묘상, 장전, 구리개 약방, 신전
피혁점, 곰보, 애꾸, 애 못 낳는 여자, 무식쟁이,
이 모든 무수한 반동이 좋다
이 땅에 발을 붙이기 위해서는
— 제삼인도교의 물 속에 박은 철근기둥도 내가 내 땅에
박는 거대한 뿌리에 비하면 좀벌레의 솜털
내가 내 땅에 박는 거대한 뿌리에 비하면

괴기영화의 맘모스를 연상시키는
까치도 까마귀도 응접을 못하는 시꺼만 가지를 가진
나도 감히 상상을 못하는 거대한 거대한 뿌리에 비하면……

Since encountering Mrs. Bishop, it is not so hard for me
to put up with Korea, rotten country though it is.
Rather, I am awed by it. History, no matter how filthy, is good.
Mud, no matter how filthy, is good.
When I have memories ringing more resonant than a
brass rice-bowl, humanity grows eternal and love likewise.

I am in love with Mrs. Bishop, the progressives and socialists
are sons of bitches, unification and neutrality are all pure shit.
Secrecy, profundity, learning, dignity, conventions, should all
go to the security agency. Oriental colonization companies,
Japanese consulates, Korean civil servants, and ice cream, too,
should all go suck American cocks; but chamber-pots,
head-bands, long pipes, nursery stores, furniture shops,
drug stores, shoe shops, leather stores, pock-marked folk,
one-eyed people, barren women, ignorant folk: all reactions
are good, in order to set foot on this land. — Comparing
the underwater beams of the third Han River bridge
with the huge roots I am putting down in my land,
they are merely the fluff on a moth's back, compared
with the huge roots I am putting down in my land.

Compared with those huge roots that even I cannot imagine,
suggestive of mammoths in horror movies,
with black boughs unable to entertain magpies or crows . . .

(February 3, 1964)

거위 소리

거위의 울음소리는
밤에도 여자의 호마색(縞瑪色) 원피스를 바람에 나부끼게 하고
강물이 흐르게 하고
꽃이 피게 하고
웃는 얼굴을 더 웃게 하고
죽은 사람을 되살아나게 한다

The Calls of Geese

The calls of geese
make a girl's white silk dress flutter even in a night breeze
make rivers flow
make flowers bloom
make laughing faces laugh more
and bring the dead to life.

(March 1964)

말

나무뿌리가 좀더 깊이 겨울을 향해 가라앉았다
이제 내 몸은 내 몸이 아니다
이 가슴의 동계(動悸)도 기침도 한기도 내것이 아니다
이 집도 아내도 아들도 어머니도 다시 내것이 아니다
오늘도 여전히 일을 하고 걱정하고
돈을 벌고 싸우고 오늘부터의 할일을 하지만
내 생명은 이미 맡기어진 생명
나의 질서는 죽음의 질서
온 세상이 죽음의 가치로 변해버렸다

익살스러울만치 모든 거리가 단축되고
익살스러울만치 모든 질문이 없어지고
모든 사람에게 고해야 할 너무나 많은 말을 갖고 있지만
세상은 나의 말에 귀를 기울이지 않는다

이 무언의 말
이때문에 아내를 다루기 어려워지고
자식을 다루기 어려워지고 친구를
다루기 어려워지고
이 너무나 큰 어려움에 나는 입을 봉하고 있는 셈이고
무서운 무성의를 자행하고 있다

이 무언의 말
하늘의 빛이요 물의 빛이요 우연(偶然)의 빛이요 우연의 말
죽음을 꿰뚫는 가장 무력한 말
죽음을 위한 말 죽음에 섬기는 말
고지식한 것을 제일 싫어하는 말

Words

The trees have sunk their roots deeper toward winter.
Now my body is no longer mine. My heart's
sudden palpitations, its colds and chills, are not mine.
House, wife, son, mother, not one is mine again.
Today, as usual, I work, and worry,
earn money, fight, and do what has to be done next
but henceforth my life has been given over,
my order belongs to the order of death,
everything has turned into the values of death.

It's ludicrous: every distance has become foreshortened,
every question has disappeared.
I find myself with too many words about things
I have to tell everyone,
but people have no ears for my words.

All these unspoken words . . .
they make it hard to deal with my wife,
they make it hard to deal with my kids, hard
to deal with my friends,
everything has got far too hard, my lips remain sealed
and I find myself resorting to dreadful insincerity.

All these unspoken words . . .
tints of heaven, tints of water, tints and words of chance,
most powerless words piercing the walls of death,
words for death, words serving death,
words utterly hating what is simple and honest,

이 만능(萬能)의 말
겨울의 말이자 봄의 말
이제 내 말은 내 말이 아니다

these words of omnipotence,
words of winter, words of spring,
now my words are no longer mine.

(November 16, 1964)

절망(絶望)

풍경이 풍경을 반성하지 않는 것처럼
곰팡이 곰팡을 반성하지 않는 것처럼
여름이 여름을 반성하지 않는 것처럼
속도가 속도를 반성하지 않는 것처럼
졸렬(拙劣)과 수치가 그들 자신을 반성하지 않는 것처럼
바람은 딴 데에서 오고
구원(救援)은 예기치 않은 순간에 오고
절망은 끝까지 그 자신을 반성하지 않는다

Despair

As a landscape never reflects upon a landscape,
as mildew never reflects upon mildew,
as summer never reflects upon summer,
as speed never reflects upon speed,
as incompetence and disgrace never reflect upon themselves,
the wind blows from elsewhere,
salvation comes when least expected,
and despair never reflects upon itself.

(August 28, 1965)

어느날 고궁을 나오면서

왜 나는 조그마한 일에만 분개하는가
저 왕궁 대신에 왕궁의 음탕 대신에
오십원짜리 갈비가 기름덩어리만 나왔다고 분개하고
옹졸하게 분개하고 설렁탕집 돼지같은 주인년한테 욕을 하고
옹졸하게 욕을 하고

한번 정정당당하게
붙잡혀간 소설가를 위해서
언론의 자유를 요구하고 월남파병에 반대하는
자유를 이행하지 못하고
이십원을 받으러 세번씩 네번씩
찾아오는 야경꾼들만 증오하고 있는가

옹졸한 나의 전통은 유구하고 이제 내 앞에 情緖로
가로놓여있다
이를테면 이런 일이 있었다
부산에 포로수용소의 제십사야전병원에 있을 때
정보원이 너어스들과 스폰지를 만들고 거즈를
개키고 있는 나를 보고 포로경찰이 되지 않는다고
남자가 뭐 이런 일을 하고 있느냐고 놀린 일이 었었다
너어스들 옆에서

지금도 내가 반항하고 있는 것은 이 스폰지 만들기와
거즈 접고 있는 일과 조금도 다름없다
개의 울음소리를 듣고 그 비명에 지고
머리에 피도 안 마른 애놈의 투정에 진다
떨어지는 은행나무잎도 내가 밟고 가는 가시밭

Emerging From an Old Palace One Day

Why do the littlest things make me livid?
Why am I not livid with that palace and its debaucheries,
but livid that I got a lump of fat for a fifty Won beef-rib,
pettily livid, swearing at the pig-like woman
in the *sollong-t'ang* restaurant, swearing pettily?

Why do I only hate the night-watchmen who come calling
three or four times to collect their twenty Won,
not once fairly and squarely
demanding freedom of expression for an imprisoned
novelist, incapable of exercising that freedom
in opposing the dispatch of forces to Vietnam?

My petty traditions, eternal as ever, stretch before me,
a structure of feelings.
For instance, something that happened
in the 14th field hospital in Pusan prison camp:
an intelligence agent, seeing me making sponges
and folding gauze pads with the nurses, mockingly said I
should be assisting the guards; what work was that for a man?
Right there in front of the nurses.

What is upsetting me now is just the same
as that sponge-making, gauze-folding.
Hearing a dog bark and surrendering to its cry.
Surrendering to the clamor of a youth, still wet behind the ears.
Even the falling ginkgo leaves are brambles
I must walk through.

아무래도 나는 비켜서있다 절정 위에는 서있지
않고 암만해도 조금쯤 옆으로 비켜서있다
그리고 조금쯤 옆에 서있는 것이 조금쯤
비겁한 것이라고 알고 있다!

그러니까 이렇게 옹졸하게 반항한다
이발쟁이에게
땅주인에게는 못하고 이발쟁이에게
구청직원에게는 못하고 동회직원에게도 못하고
야경꾼에게 이십원 때문에 십원 때문에 일원 때문에
우습지 않느냐 일원 때문에

모래야 나는 얼마큼 적으냐
바람아 먼지야 풀아 나는 얼마큼 적으냐
정말 얼마큼 적으냐……

I am standing aside; indeed, I never stand right at the top
but move a bit to one side. Yet I know
that standing a bit to one side
is a slightly cowardly deed!

So here I am, petty and livid.
Livid with the barber, since I can't be livid with the landlord;
livid with the barber, since I can't be livid
with officials high or low in the local government offices;
livid with the night-watchmen, for twenty Won, for ten Won,
for one, isn't it ridiculous? For one single Won.

Tell me, sand: how small am I?
Wind, dust, grass, tell me: how small am I?
Really, now, how small?

(November 4, 1965)

눈

눈이 온 뒤에도 또 내린다

생각하고 난 뒤에도 또 내린다

응아 하고 운 뒤에도 또 내릴까

한꺼번에 생각하고 또 내린다

한줄 건너 두줄 건너 또 내릴까

폐허(廢墟)에 폐허에 눈이 내릴까

Snow

After snow has fallen, it keeps falling.

After a thought has occurred, it keeps falling.

After a wail, will it keep falling?

After a sudden thought, it keeps falling.

One line passed, two lines passed, will it keep falling?

Will snow fall on ruins, on ruins?

(January 29, 1966)

네 얼굴은

네 얼굴은 진리에 도달했다
어저께 진리에 도달했다
어저께 환희를 잃었기 때문이다

아아 보기싫은 머리에 두툼한 어깨는
허위(虛僞)의 상징
꺼져라 이십년 전의 악마야

손에는 무거운 보따리를 들고
가다가다 기침을 하면서
집에는 차압을 해온 빠일오바가 있는데도
배자 위에 얄따란 검정오바를 입고
사흘 전에 술에 취해 흘린 가래침 자국 —
아니 빚장이와 싸우다 나오는 길에 흘린
침자국

죽어라 이성을 되찾기 전에

네 얼굴은 진리에 도달했다
어저께 진리에 도달한 얼굴은
오늘은 술을 잊은 얼굴이다

가구점의 문앞에서 책꽂이를
묶어주는 철쭉꽃빛 루즈를 바른
주인여자의 얼굴 —
그 얼굴은 네 얼굴보다는
간음을 상상할 수 있을만큼
그렇게 조금은 생생하지만

Your Face

Your face attained the truth,
yesterday attained the truth,
for yesterday you lost delight.

What thick shoulders beneath that disgusting head:
symbols of falsehood.
Down with the devil of twenty years past!

A heavy bundle in your hand,
you go walking coughing on and on;
your thick coat sequestered back at home,
a thin black coat thrown over your bodice,
phlegm-smeared from when you got drunk three days ago —
or spittle
dribbled after you fought the loan shark.

Die before you regain your senses.

Your face attained the truth.
The face that yesterday attained the truth
is a face that today has forgotten drink.

Out in front of the furniture store,
busy wrapping bookshelves, her lips azalea-red,
the face of the store owner's wife —
more capable than yours
of adulterous thoughts, a bit more lively;

죽어라 돈을 받기보다는
죽어라 돈을 받기 전에

but die rather than take money,
die before you ever take money.

사랑의 변주곡(變奏曲)

욕망이여 입을 열어라 그 속에서
사랑을 발견하겠다 도시의 끝에
사그러져가는 라디오의 재갈거리는 소리가
사랑처럼 들리고 그 소리가 지워지는
강이 흐르고 그 강건너에 사랑하는
암흑이 있고 삼월을 바라보는 마른나무들이
사랑의 봉오리를 준비하고 그 봉오리의
속삭임이 안개처럼 이는 저쪽에 쪽빛
산이

사랑의 기차가 지나갈 때마다 우리들의
슬픔처럼 자라나고 도야지우리의 밥찌끼
같은 서울의 등불을 무시한다
이제 가시밭, 덩쿨장미의 기나긴 가시가지
까지도 사랑이다

왜 이렇게 벅차게 사랑의 숲은 밀려닥치느냐
사랑의 음식이 사랑이라는 것을 알 때까지

난로 위에 끓어오르는 주전자의 물이 아슬
아슬하게 넘지 않는 것처럼 사랑의 절도(節度)는
열렬하다
간단(間斷)도 사랑
이 방에서 저 방으로 할머니가 계신 방에서
심부름하는 놈이 있는 방까지 죽음같은
암흑 속을 고양이의 반짝거리는 푸른 눈망울처럼
사랑이 이어져가는 밤을 안다
그리고 이 사랑을 만드는 기술을 안다

Variations on the Theme of Love

Open your lips, Desire, and within
I will discover love. At the city limits
the sound of the fading radio's chatter
sounds like love while the river flows on,
drowning it, and on the far shore lies
loving darkness while dry trees, beholding March,
prepare love's buds and the whispers
of those buds rise like mists across yon indigo
mountains

Every time love's train passes by
the mountains grow like our sorrow and ignore
the lamplight of Seoul like the remnants of food in a pigsty.
Now even brambles, even the long thorny runners
of rambling roses are love.

Why does love's grove come pushing so impossibly near?
Until we realize that loving is the food of love.

Just as water in a kettle boiling on a stove
nearly spills over but not quite, love's moderation
is a torrid thing.
Interruption is love, too.
I know nights when love persists
like the green eyes of a cat shining in
death-like darkness, from this room to that,
from grandma's room to the room of the errand-boy.
And I know the art of producing such love.

눈을 떴다 감는 기술—불란서혁명의 기술
최근 우리들이 사·일구에서 배운 기술
그러나 이제 우리들은 소리내어 외치지 않는다

복사씨와 살구씨와 곶감씨의 아름다운 단단함이여
고요함과 사랑이 이루어놓은 폭풍(暴風)의 간악한
신념(信念)이여
봄베이도 뉴욕도 서울도 마찬가지다
신념보다도 더 큰
내가 묻혀사는 사랑의 위대한 도시에 비하면
너는 개미이냐

아들아 너에게 광신(狂信)을 가르치기 위한 것이 아니다
사랑을 알 때까지 자라라
인류의 종언의 날에
너의 술을 다 마시고 난 날에
미대륙에서 석유가 고갈되는 날에
그렇게 먼 날까지 가기 전에 너의 가슴에
새겨둘 말을 너는 도시의 피로(疲勞)에서
배울 거다
이 단단한 고요함을 배울 거다
복사씨가 사랑으로 만들어진 것이 아닌가 하고
의심할 거다!
복사씨와 살구씨가
한번은 이렇게
사랑에 미쳐 날뜀 날이 올 거다!
그리고 그것은 아버지같은 잘못된 시간의
그릇된 명상(瞑想)이 아닐 거다

The art of opening and closing eyes — the art
of the French Revolution, the art we learned on April 19,
but now we never shout.

Lovely firmness of peach seeds, apricot seeds,
dry persimmon seeds.
Wicked faith of the storm stirred up by silence and love,
the same in Pompeii, New York, and in Seoul.
Compared to the vast city of love I am burying,
greater even than faith,
aren't you a mere ant?

My son, this is not designed to teach you fanaticism.
Grow up until you come to know love.
Humanity's final moments,
the day you drink your cup to the dregs,
the day America's oil dries up:
before you reach such distant times, the words
you will register in your heart are words you will learn
from the city's fatigue.
You will learn this firm silence.
You will wonder whether
the peach seed is not made of love!
Sometime the day will come
when peach seed and apricot seed
will leap up, maddened by love!
And that will not be the false meditation
of a mistaken hour like your father's.

(February 2, 1967)

꽃잎 (一)

누구한테 머리를 숙일까
사람이 아닌 평범한 것에
많이는 아니고 조금
벼를 터는 마당에서 바람도 안 부는데
옥수수잎이 흔들리듯 그렇게 조금

바람의 고개는 자기가 일어서는줄
모르고 자기가 가닿는 언덕을
모르고 거룩한 산에 가닿기
전에는 즐거움을 모르고 조금
안 즐거움이 꽃으로 되어도
그저 조금 꺼졌다 깨어나고

언뜻 보기엔 임종의 생명같고
바위를 뭉개고 떨어져내릴
한 잎의 꽃잎같고
혁명같고
먼저 떨어져내린 큰 바위같고
나중에 떨어진 작은 꽃잎같고

나중에 떨어져내린 작은 꽃잎같고

Petal   1

Who shall I bow to?
To ordinary non-human things,
not too much, just a little,
as little as when maize leaves shake
though no wind blows on the threshing-floor.

The wind's brow unaware
of having risen, unaware
of the hills it touches, unaware
of joy before it touches holy mountains,
though the little joy it knows become a flower,
it fades a little, then revives,

to a casual eye like life at death's door,
like a single petal
about to fall after shattering rocks,
like revolution,
like huge rocks already fallen,
like a tiny petal that later fell

like a tiny petal that later fell.

(May 2, 1967)

꽃잎 (二)

꽃을 주세요 우리의 고뇌를 위해서
꽃을 주세요 뜻밖의 일을 위해서
꽃을 주세요 아까와는 다른 시간을 위해서

노란 꽃을 주세요 금이 간 꽃을
노란 꽃을 주세요 하얘져가는 꽃을
노란 꽃을 주세요 넓어져가는 소란을

노란 꽃을 받으세요 원수를 지우기 위해서
노란 꽃을 받으세요 우리가 아닌 것을 위해서
노란 꽃을 받으세요 거룩한 우연을 위해서

꽃을 찾기 전의 것을 잊어버리세요
　꽃의 글자가 비뚤어지지 않게
꽃을 찾기 전의 것을 잊어버리세요
　꽃의 소음이 바로 들어오게
꽃을 찾기 전의 것을 잊어버리세요
　꽃의 글자가 다시 비뚤어지게

내 말을 믿으세요 노란 꽃을
못 보는 글자를 믿으세요 노란 꽃을
떨리는 글자를 믿으세요 노란 꽃을
영원히 떨리면서 빼먹은 모든 꽃잎을 믿으세요
보기싫은 노란 꽃을

Petal   2

Give flowers for our anguish
Give flowers for unexpected events
Give flowers for time unlike before

Give yellow flowers, flowers that have cracked
Give yellow flowers, flowers fading to white
Give yellow flowers, commotion spreading wide

Take yellow flowers to overcome enemies
Take yellow flowers for things not ourselves
Take yellow flowers for sacred chance

Forget the things before you found flowers
        So the flowers' writing does not grow crooked
Forget the things before you found flowers
        So the flowers' noise enters straight in
Forget the things before you found flowers
        So the flowers' writing grows crooked again

Believe what I say: yellow flowers
Believe the invisible writing: yellow flowers
Believe the quaking writing: yellow flowers
Believe all the petals eternally quaking omitted
Disgusting yellow flowers

(May 7, 1967)

여름밤

지상의 소음이 번성하는 날은
하늘의 소음도 번쩍인다
여름은 이래서 좋고 여름밤은
이래서 더욱 좋다

소음에 시달린 마당 한구석에
철늦게 핀 여름장미의 흰구름
소나기가 지나고 바람이 불듯
하더니 또 안 불고
소음은 더욱 번성해진다

사람이 사람을 아끼는 날
소음이 더욱 번성하다 남은 날
사람이 사람을 사랑하던 날
소음이 더욱 번성하기 전날
우리는 언제나 소음의 이층

땅의 이층이 하늘인 것처럼
이렇게 인정의 하늘이 가까워진
일이 없다 남을 불쌍히 생각함은
나를 불쌍히 생각함이라
나와 또 나의 아들까지도

사람이 사람을 사랑하다 남은 날
땅에만 소음이 있는줄만 알았더니
하늘에도 천둥이, 우리의 귀가
들을 수 없는 더 큰 천둥이 있는줄
알았다 그것이 먼저 있는줄 알았다

Summer Nights

On days when terrestrial noise flourishes,
heavenly noise glitters bright as well.
So summer is good,
summer nights are even better.

In one corner of the garden vexed by noise
a white cloud of summer roses blossoms late,
a shower passes,
breezes seem to blow
yet then again not to blow; noise flourishes even more.

On days when people treasure others,
on days when noise flourishes still more and remains,
on days when people have loved others,
on days before days when noise flourishes more,
we are always at noise's second level.

Just as earth's second level seems like heaven,
nothing can bring the heaven of kindness
so close. Feeling sorry for others
is feeling sorry for myself.
For me and for my son as well.

On days when people love others and keep doing so,
I used to consider there was noise only on earth
but then I realized there was thunder in heaven,
a louder thunder that our ears cannot hear; I realized that
that was there first.

지상의 소음이 번성하는 날은
하늘의 천둥도 번쩍인다
여름밤은 깊을수록
이래서 좋아진다

On days when terrestrial noise flourishes,
heavenly thunder glitters bright as well.
As summer nights grow darker,
they grow better, too.

(July 27, 1967)

풀

풀이 눕는다
비를 몰아오는 동풍에 나부껴
풀은 눕고
드디어 울었다
날이 흐려서 더 울다가
다시 누웠다

풀이 눕는다
바람보다도 더 빨리 눕는다
바람보다도 더 빨리 울고
바람보다 먼저 일어난다

날이 흐리고 풀이 눕는다
발목까지
발밑까지 눕는다
바람보다 늦게 누워도
바람보다 먼저 일어나고
바람보다 늦게 울어도
바람보다 먼저 웃는다
날이 흐르고 풀뿌리가 눕는다

Grass

The grass is lying flat.
Fluttering in the east wind that brings rain in its train,
the grass lay flat
and at last it wept.
As the day grew cloudier, it wept even more
and lay flat again.

The grass is lying flat.
It lies flat more quickly than the wind.
It weeps more quickly than the wind.
It rises more quickly than the wind.

The day is cloudy, the grass is lying flat.
It lies low as the ankles
low as the feet.
Though it lies flat later than the wind,
it rises more quickly than the wind
and though it weeps later than the wind,
it laughs more quickly than the wind.
The day is cloudy, the grass's roots are lying flat.

(May 29, 1968)

Shin Kyong-Nim
신 경림

Shin Kyong-Nim (Kyǒng-Nim) was born in 1935. His literary career dates from the publication of three poems, including 갈대 *The Reed*, in 1956 but after that he published nothing for a number of years, immersing himself instead in the world of the working classes, the *"Minjung,"* and working as a farmer, a miner, and a merchant. His fame dates mainly from the publication of his first collection, 農舞 *Nong-mu* (*Farmers' Dance*), in 1973. Shin Kyong-Nim has continued to play a leading role in the world of socially involved poetry. He has served as president of the Association of Writers for National Literature, and of the Federated Union of Korean Nationalist Artists.

Other volumes of his poetry include 새재 *Saejae* (1979), 달넘세 *Talnǒmse* (1985), 남한강 *Namhankang* (*South Han River*, 1987), 가난한 사랑 노래 *Kana nhan sarangnorae* (*Song of poor love*, 1988), 길 *Kil* (*Road*, 1990), 쓰러진 자의 꿈 *Ssǔrǒjin cha ǔi kkum* (Dreams of the fallen, 1993), 할머니와 어머니의 실 우에트 *Halmǒn i wa ǒmǒni ǔi silhouette* (*Silhouettes of grandmother and mother*, 1998). This last volume received the 1998 Daesan Literary Award for Poetry. It was published too recently to be included here. He has also published several collections of literary and personal essays.

He has traveled widely collecting the popular songs that have survived in Korea's rural areas and his poetry is deeply marked by the rhythms of traditional Korean music as a result.

An English translation of *Farmers' Dance* was published in this same series in 1999.

겨울밤

우리는 협동조합 방앗간 뒷방에 모여
묵내기 화투를 치고
내일은 장날. 장꾼들은 왁자지껄
주막집 뜰에서 눈을 턴다.
들과 산은 온통 새하얗구나. 눈은
펑펑 쏟아지는데
쌀값 비료값 얘기가 나오고
선생이 된 면장 딸 얘기가 나오고.
서울로 식모살이 간 분이는
아기를 뱄다더라. 어떡할거나.
술에라도 취해볼거나. 술집 색시
싸구려 분 냄새라도 맡아볼거나.
우리의 슬픔을 아는 것은 우리뿐.
올해에는 닭이라도 쳐볼거나.
겨울밤은 길어 묵을 먹고.
술을 마시고 물세 시비를 하고
색시 젓갈 장단에 유행가를 부르고
이발소집 신랑을 다루러
보리밭을 질러가면 세상은 온통
하얗구나. 눈이여 쌓여
지붕을 덮어다오 우리를 파묻어다오.
오종대 뒤에 치마를 둘러쓰고
숨은 저 계집애들한테
연애편지라도 띄워볼거나. 우리의
괴로움을 아는 것은 우리뿐.
올해에는 돼지라도 먹여볼거나.

On a Winter's Night

We're met in the back room of the co-op mill
playing cards for a dish of *muk*;
tomorrow's market-day. Boisterous merchants
shake off the snow in the inn's front yard.
Fields and hills shine newly white, the falling snow
comes swirling thickly down.
People are talking about the price of rice and fertilizers,
and about the local magistrate's daughter, a teacher.
Hey, it seems Puni, up in Seoul working as a maid,
is going to have a baby. Well, what shall we do?
Shall we get drunk? The bar-girl smells
of cheap powder, but still, shall we have a sniff?
We're the only ones who know our sorrows.
Shall we try raising fowls this year?
Winter nights are long, we eat *muk*,
down drinks, argue over the water rates,
sing to the bar-girl's chop-stick beat,
and as we cross the barley-field to give a hard time
to the newly-wed man at the barber's shop,
look at that: the world's all white. Come on snow, drift high,
high as the roof, bury us deep.
Shall we send a love-letter
to those girls behind the siren tower hiding
wrapped in their skirts? We're
the only ones who know our troubles.
Shall we try fattening pigs this year?

파장 (罷場)

못난 놈들은 서로 얼굴만 봐도 흥겹다
이발소 앞에 서서 참외를 깎고
목로에 앉아 막걸리를 들이켜면
모두들 한결같이 친구 같은 얼굴들
호남의 가뭄 얘기 조합빚 얘기
약장수 기타소리에 발장단을 치다 보면
왜 이렇게 자꾸만 서울이 그리워지나
어디를 들어가 섰다라도 벌일까
주머니를 털어 색싯집에라도 갈까
학교 마당에들 모여 소주에 오징어를 찢다
어느새 긴 여름해도 저물어
고무신 한 켤레 또는 조기 한 마리 들고
달이 환한 마찻길을 절뚝이는 파장

After Market's Done

We plain folk are happy just to see each other.
Peeling *ch'amoi* melons in front of the barber's,
gulping *makkolli* at the bar,
all our faces invariably like those of friends,
talking of drought down south, or of co-op debts,
keeping time with our feet to the herb peddler's guitar.
Why are we all the time longing for Seoul?
Shall we go somewhere and gamble at cards?
Shall we empty our purses and go to the whore-house?
We gather in the school-yard, munch strips of squid with *soju*.
In no time at all the long summer day's done
and off we go down the bright moonlit cart-track
carrying a pair of rubber shoes or a single croaker,
staggering home after market's done.

농무 (農舞)

징이 울린다 막이 내렸다
오동나무에 전등이 매어달린 가설무대
구경꾼이 돌아가고 난 텅 빈 운동장
우리는 분이 얼룩진 얼굴로
학교 앞 소줏집에 몰려 술을 마신다
답답하고 고달프게 사는 것이 원통하다
꽹과리를 앞장 세워 장거리로 나서면
따라붙어 악을 쓰는 건 쪼무래기들뿐
처녀애들은 기름집 담벽에 붙어서서
철없이 킬킬대는구나
보름달은 밝아 어떤 녀석은
꺽정이처럼 울부짖고 또 어떤 녀석은
서림이처럼 해해대지만 이까짓
산구석에 처박혀 발버둥친들 무엇하랴
비료값도 안 나오는 농사 따위야
아예 여편네에게나 맡겨두고
쇠전을 거쳐 도수장 앞에 와 돌 때
우리는 점점 신명이 난다
한 다리를 들고 날라리를 불거나
고갯짓을 하고 어깨를 흔들거나

Farmers' Dance

The *ching* rings out, the curtain falls.
Above the rough stage, lights dangle from a paulownia tree,
the playground's empty, everyone's gone home.
We rush to the *soju* bar in front of the school
and drink, our faces still daubed with powder.
Life's mortifying when you're oppressed and wretched.
Then off down the market alleys behind the *kkwenggwari*
with only some kids running bellowing behind us
while girls lean pressed against the oil shop wall
giggling childish giggles.
The full moon rises and one of us
begins to wail like the bandit king Kkokchong; another
laughs himself sly like Sorim the schemer; after all
what's the use of fretting and struggling, shut up in these hills
with farming not paying the fertilizer bills?
Leaving it all in the hands of the women,
we pass by the cattle-fair,
then dancing in front of the slaughterhouse
we start to get into the swing of things.
Shall we dance on one leg, blow the *nallari* hard?
Shall we shake our heads, make our shoulders rock?

그 겨울

진눈깨비가 흩뿌리는 금방앗간
그 아랫말 마찻집 사랑채에
우리는 쌀 너 말씩에 밥을 붙였다.
연상도 덕대도 명일 쇠러 가 없고
절벽 사이로 몰아치는 바람은 지겨워
종일 참나무불 쇠화로를 끼고 앉아
제천역전 앞 하숙집에서 만난
영자라던 그 어린 갈보 얘기를 했다.
때로는 과부집으로 몰려가
외상 돼지 도로리에 한몫 끼였다.
진눈깨비가 더욱 기승을 부리는 보름께면
객지로 돈벌이 갔던 마찻집 손자가
알거지가 되어 돌아와 그를 위해
술판이 벌어지는 것이지만
그 술판은 이내 싸움판으로 변했다.
부락 청년들과 한산 인부들은
서로 패를 갈라 주먹을 휘두르고
박치기를 하고 그릇을 내던졌다.
이 못난 짓은 오래가지는 않아
이내 뉘우치고 울음을 터뜨리고
새 술판을 차려 육자배기로 돌렸다.
그러다 주먹들을 부르쥐고 밖으로 나오면
식모살이들을 가 처녀 하나 남지 않은
골짜기 광산 부락은 그대로 칠흑이었다.
쓰러지고 엎어지면서 우리들은
노래를 불러댔다. 개가 짖고 닭이
울어도 겁나지 않는 첫새벽
진눈깨비는 이제 함박눈으로 바뀌고
산비탈길은 빙판이 져 미끄러웠다.

That Winter

Sleet filtered down over the gold mill and
in the guest-room of the carrier's just below it
we boarded for four bushels of rice each.
Yon-sang and Tok-taek had gone home to celebrate
the holidays, the wind driving past the cliffs was grim and
all day we sat hugging the iron stove with its oak wood fire
talking about a kid whore called Yongja
we'd met at a boarding-house in front of Chech'on station.
Sometimes we went rushing off to the widow's tavern
for a bite of pork that we chipped in to buy on credit.
At about full moon, when heavier sleets always fell,
the carrier's grandson, who'd gone away to make his fortune,
came back even poorer than before and
we held a party for him to celebrate only
the party soon turned into a fight.
The village lads and the laborers from Hansan
divided into gangs and traded blows,
knocked heads together, threw dishes about.
The unseemly conduct didn't last long;
soon they were sorry and burst into tears, began a new party,
passing glasses round to the *Yukchabegi* beat.
When we clenched our fists and stepped outside
the valley mining village was dark as pitch; there was
not one girl left, all were off working as housemaids.
Falling down, tumbling about, we
bellowed out songs. At first light
we were not afraid though dogs barked and cocks crowed,
the sleet had now turned into a solid snowfall,
the mountain paths were treacherous, slippery with ice.

갈대

언제부턴가 갈대는 속으로
조용히 울고 있었다.
그런 어느 밤이었을 것이다. 갈대는
그의 온몸이 흔들리고 있는 것을 알았다.

바람도 달빛도 아닌 것.
갈대는 저를 흔드는 것이 제 조용한 울음인 것을
까맣게 몰랐다.
— 산다는 것은 속으로 이렇게
조용히 울고 있는 것이란 것을
그는 몰랐다.

A Reed

For some time past, a reed had been
quietly weeping inwardly.
Then finally, one evening, the reed
realized it was trembling all over.

It wasn't the wind or the moon.
The reed was utterly unaware that it was its own
quiet inward weeping that was making it tremble
    — It was unaware
that being alive is a matter
of quiet inward weeping.

목계장터

하늘은 날더러 구름이 되라 하고
땅은 날더러 바람이 되라 하네
청룡 흑룡 흩어져 비 개인 나루
잡초나 일깨우는 잔바람이 되라네
뱃길이라 서울 사흘 목계 나루에
아흐레 나흘 찾아 박가분 파는
가을볕도 서러운 방물장수 되라네
산은 날더러 들꽃이 되라 하고
강은 날더러 잔돌이 되라 하네
산서리 맵차거든 풀 속에 얼굴 묻고
물여울 모질거든 바위 뒤에 붙으라네
민물 새우 끓어넘는 토방 툇마루
석삼년에 한 이레쯤 천치로 변해
짐부리고 앉아 쉬는 떠돌이가 되라네
하늘은 날더러 바람이 되라 하고
산은 날더러 잔돌이 되라 하네

Mokkye Market

The sky urges me to turn into a cloud,
the earth urges me to turn into a breeze,
a little breeze waking weeds on the ferry landing
once storm clouds have scattered and rain has cleared.
To turn into a peddler sad even in autumn light,
going to Mokkye Ferry, three days' boat ride from Seoul,
to sell patent face-powders, on days four and nine.
The hills urge me to turn into a flower,
the stream urges me to turn into a stone.
To hide my face in the grass when hoarfrost bites,
to wedge behind rocks when rapids rage cruel.
To turn into a traveler with pack laid by, resting
on a clay hovel's wood step, river shrimps boiling up,
changed into a fool for a week or so, once in thrice three years.
The sky urges me to turn into a breeze,
the hills urge me to turn into a stone.

4월 19일, 시골에 와서

밤새워 문짝이 덜컹대고
골목을 축축한 바람이 쓸고 있다.
헐린 담장에 어수선한 두엄더미 위에
살구꽃이 피고 어지럽게
피어서 꺾이고 밟히고
그래도 다시 피는 4월.

나는 남한강 상류 외진 읍내에 와서
통금이 없는 빈 거리를 헤매이며
어느새 잊어버린
그날의 함성을 생각했다.
티끌처럼 쏠리며 살아온 나날.
돌처럼 뒹굴며 이어온 세월.

다시 그날의 종소리가 들리리라고
아무도 믿지 않는 밤은 어두웠다.
친구를 생각했다. 찬 돌에 이마를 대고
깊은 잠이 들었을 친구를
그 손톱에 배었을 핏자국을.

4월이 와도 바람은 그냥 차고
살구꽃이 피어도 흐느낌은 더 높은데
축축한 바람은 꽃가지에 와 매달려
친구들의 울음처럼 잉잉댔다.
진달래도 개나리도 피고
꺾이고 밟히고 다시 피는 4월
밤은 좀체 밝아오지 않았다.

A Country Village, April 19

The door has been rattling all night long
in the damp breeze sweeping down the alley.
Over the messy dung-heap by the broken-down wall
apricot flowers are in bloom, dizzyingly
they bloom, get plucked off, trodden down,
yet they bloom again, it's April.

I had reached a lonely village high up on the South Han River,
and as I wandered down empty streets free of curfew,
all at once the forgotten
battle cries of that day came to mind.
The days lived since then slant like motes of dust.
Time has passed like a rolling stone.

The night was dark, no one believed
we would ever hear that day's bells again.
I recalled a friend, his brow struck by a cold stone,
a friend fallen into so deep sleep,
blood staining his finger-nails.

It might be April, the wind was still chill,
despite apricot flowers, the sobs rose higher,
the damp breeze came clinging to the flowering branches,
whimpering like those friends' laments.
Azaleas bloom, and forsythias too, they get plucked off,
trodden down, yet they bloom again, it's April.
The night hardly grew any brighter.

개치 나루에서

이곳은 내 진외가가 살던 고장이다
그 해 봄에 꽃가루가 날리고
꽃바람 타고 역병이 찾아와
마을과 나루가 죽음으로 덮이던 고장이다

다시 전쟁이 일어
내 외로운 친구 숨죽여 떠돌다가
저 느티나무 아래
몰매로 묻힌 고장이다

바람아 다 잊었구나
늙은 나무에 굵은 살구꽃이 달려도
봄이 와서 내 친구 꽃에 붙어 울어도
바람아 너는 잊었구나 그 이름
그 한 그 설움을

이곳은 내 진외가가 살던 고장이지만
죽음 위에 꽃가루 날리던 나루이지만
원통하게 내 친구 묻힌 고장이지만
모두 다 잊어버린 장바닥을 돌다
한산한 대합실 나무의자에 앉아
읍내로 가는 시외버스를 기다린다
바람아 너는 잊었구나 그 이름
그 한 그 설움을

At Kech'i Landing Stage

This place was once my grandmother's home.
Pollen was drifting in the spring that year,
when pestilence came riding on the flowery breeze;
her home was a village and a landing decked with death.

Then wartime came again
and this is the place where my lonely friend
wandered stealthily a while, then was stoned
and at last was buried at the foot of that zelkova tree.

Ah breeze, you have forgotten it all.
Thick apricot blossoms speed toward the old tree,
spring comes and my friend laments united with them,
yet you, ah breeze, have forgotten it all: the name,
the bitterness, the grief.

This place was once my grandmother's home,
a landing where once pollen drifted over death,
the place where, alas, my friend was buried; but now
I'm sitting on a wooden bench in the silent bus-station, waiting
for a bus to the nearby town,
after strolling around the market place, that has forgotten it all.
Ah breeze, you have forgotten it all too: the name,
the bitterness, the grief.

나는 부끄러웠다 어린 누이야

차고 누진 네 방에 낡은 옷가지들
라면 봉지와 쭈그러진 냄비
나는 부끄러웠다 어린 누이야
너희들의 힘으로 살쪄가는 거리
너희들의 땀으로 기름져 가는 도시
오히려 그것들이 너희들을 조롱하고
오직 가난만이 죄악이라 협박할 때
나는 부끄러웠다 어린 누이야
벚꽃이 활짝 핀 공장 담벽 안
후지레한 초록색 작업복에 감겨
꿈 대신 분노의 눈물을 삼킬 때
나는 부끄러웠다 어린 누이야
투박한 손마디에 얼룩진 기름때
빛 바랜 네 얼굴에 생활의 흠집
야윈 어깨에 밴 삶의 어려움
나는 부끄러웠다 어린 누이야
나는 부끄러웠다 어린 누이야
우리들 두려워 얼굴 숙이고
시골 장바닥 뒷골목에 처박혀
그 한겨우내 술놀음 허송 속에
네 울부짖음만이 온 마을을 덮었을 때
들을 메우고 산과 하늘에 넘칠 때
쓰러지고 짓밟히고 다시 일어설 때
네 투박한 손에 힘을 보았을 때
네 빛 바랜 얼굴에 참삶을 보았을 때
네 야윈 어깨에 꿈을 보았을 때
나는 부끄러웠다 어린 누이야
네 울부짖음 속에 내일을 보았을 때
네 노랫속에 빛을 보았을 때

I Felt Ashamed, Little Sisters

I felt ashamed, little sisters,
of the old clothes in your cold damp room,
the packs of *ramyon* noodles and the battered pans.
When the streets grew fat by your efforts
and the city grew sleek at the expense of your sweat,
and they simply mocked you
and forced you to admit that poverty is the only crime,
I felt ashamed, little sisters.
When dressed in flabby green working clothes
behind factory walls bright with cherry-flowers
you choked back tears of wrath, in place of dreams,
I felt ashamed, little sisters.
At the grease all staining your rough hands,
the scars left by life on your pale faded cheeks,
the hardships of life borne on your gaunt shoulders,
I felt ashamed, little sisters.
I felt ashamed, little sisters.
We were afraid, we hid out faces, all winter long
we wasted our time at gambling and drink,
shut up in the back-alleys of that market village.
When naught but your screams covered the whole village,
when they filled the meadows, passed hills and sky,
when you fell, were trampled, and rose up again,
when I saw strength in your rough hands,
when I saw a true and honest life in your pale faded cheeks,
when I saw dreams on your gaunt shoulders,
I felt ashamed, little sisters,
when I saw tomorrow within your screams,
when I saw light within your songs.

옥대문 (玉大門)

하얀병 던져라 열두 강 갈라지고
노랑병 던져라 불바다 재가 되네
열려라 돌대문 참흙 거적 위
내 아이들 무릎 안고 새벽잠이 든.
아이들 들쳐업고 열두 강을 건넜네
뇌성벽력 여우꾐에 혼이 빠져도
바위에 찢기고 가시에 긁히면서
빨강병 던졌네 불바다 다시 열어
파랑병 던졌네 열두 강 도로 막혀.
동네 밖에 금줄 쳐 잡귀 막아 놓고
닫혀라 옥대문 떡갈나무 밑
내 아이들 새소리에 눈뜨는 아침.

투전방 뒷전에서 빨강병을 얻었네
떠돌이 책전에서 파랑병을 얻었네
헐린 시골 정거장 대목밑 장날
눈먼 계집 장타령에 노랑병을 얻었네.
강물을 가르고 불바다 지나
돌대문 열고 가서 내 아이들 업었네.
닫혀라 옥대문 눈뜬 내 아이들
머리 한 올 바람조차 넘볼 수 없게.

Gates of Jade

Cast in a white flask, and the twelve rivers divide,
cast in a yellow flask, and the oceans of fire turn to ash.
Open now, Gates of Stone; my children are sleeping
their daybreak sleep, clasping their knees on arrowroot mats.
I crossed the twelve rivers bearing my children on my back.
Though my spirit succumbed to thunder and temptation
by foxes, and was rent on rocks, torn by thorns,
I cast in a scarlet flask, the ocean of fire gaped open again;
I cast in a turquoise flask,
    twelve rivers blocked the path behind.
Outside the village, I fended off spirits with a festoon of straw.
Now close, Gates of Jade; my children are opening their eyes
to bird-song beneath an oak tree.

The scarlet flask I got from behind a gambling den;
the turquoise flask I got from a wandering bookseller;
the yellow flask I got from a blind girl's song
at a ruined village bus-station on a main market day.
I divided the rivers, crossed the oceans of fire,
opened the Gate of Stone and bore my children through.
Now close, Gates of Jade. My children have opened their eyes;
let the wind not hurt one hair on their heads.

찔레꽃

아카샤 꽃냄새가 진한 과수원 샛길을
처녀애들이 기운없이 걷고 있었다
먼지가 켜로 앉은 이파리 사이로
멀리 실공장이 보이고 행진곡이 들리고
기름과 오물로 더럽혀진 냇물에서
아이들이 병든 고기를 잡고 있었다
나는 한 그루 찔레꽃을 찾고 있었다
가라앉은 어둠 번지는 종소리
보리 팬 언덕 그 소녀를 찾고 있었다
보도는 불을 뿜고 가뭄은 목을 태워
마주치면 사람들은 눈길을 피했다
겨울은 아직 멀다지만 죽음은 다가오고
플라타나스도 미류나무도 누렇게 썩었다
늙은이들은 잘린 느티나무에 붙어앉아
깊고 지친 기침들을 하는데
오직 한 그루 찔레꽃이 피어 있었다
냇가 허물어진 방죽 아래 숨어 서서
다가오는 죽음의 발자욱을 울고 있었다

A Dog-rose

The little girls were walking listlessly along the paths
in orchards thick with the scent of acacia flowers.
In the distance, between thickly dust-strewn leaves
the spinning mill was visible, a march could be heard,
and in the stream filthy with oil and muck
children were catching sickly fish.
I was searching for a branch of dog-roses.
The sound of a bell, the spreading darkness,
the barley-thick hill; I was searching for the little girls.
The path was burning hot, scorched by drought;
people turned their eyes aside when we happened to meet.
Death was close, though they said winter was still far off,
plane trees and poplars were fading into yellow.
The old folks were sitting against the hacked off zelkova
coughing deeply, wearily,
and only a single dog-rose was blooming.
Hidden beneath the stream's crumbling bank,
it was mourning the footprints of approaching death.

오지일기 (奧地日記)

거리에는 아직 가을볕이 따가웠다.
수수밭에 바람이 일고
미류나무가 누렇게 퇴색해도
활석광산으로 가는 트럭이 온 읍내를
먼지로 뒤덮는 추분.

그 탁한 먼지 속에서 나는
한 여자를 알게 되었다.
우리는 사랑을 하게 되었나보다
지치고 맥빠진 그 따분한 사랑을.

사과가 익는 과수원을 돌아
거기 연못을 찾아가면 여자는 이내
말을 잃고 나는 그 곁에서
쓴 막소주를 마셨다.

어디에도 내 친구들은 없었다.
연못 위에는 낮달이 떴으나
떠도는 것은 숱한 원귀들뿐이었다.
여자는 더욱 말을 잃었지만

삶은 갈수록 답답하고 가을이 와도
읍내는 온통 먼지로 뒤덮였다.
물가 술집 마루에 와 앉으면
참빗장수들 구성진 노랫가락
물바람 타고 오고

바라보면 멀리 뻗친 고갯길

Up-country Diary

In the streets, the autumn wind was still scorching.
In the millet fields the wind was rising
and the poplars were fading into yellow,
while the trucks on their way to the talc mine
smothered the town with dust: it was the autumn equinox.

In the thick of all that dust I
made the acquaintance of a girl.
It seems we fell in love:
a weary, languid, lifeless kind of love.

Once we reached the lily pond on the far side
of the orchard full of ripening apples, the girl
suddenly lost her tongue, while I sat beside her
drinking bitter *soju*.

I had no friends anywhere.
A daytime moon had risen over the pond
but the only things on the move were all those ghosts.
The girl fell more silent than ever.

As life goes on it only gets worse, and even in autumn
the town was all the time smothered in that dust.
We sat down on the wooden porch of a waterside tavern,
where the elegant songs of bamboo comb merchants
sailed to and fro on the river breeze.

Looking up, the hill road stretched into the distance

타박대는 외지 장꾼들 또 일소들.
여자의 치마에 개흙이 묻어 돌아오는
미류나무가 누렇게 퇴색한 언덕길에서

우리는 사랑을 하게 되었나보다
지치고 맥빠진 그 따분한 사랑을.
수수밭에 바람이 일고 추분이 와도
거리에도 지붕에도 간판에도 가슴에도
온통 뿌옇게 먼지만 쌓였다.

with plodding peddlers from far away, and beasts of burden.
The girl's skirt was smeared with mud; on our way back
over the hill road with poplars faded and yellow

it seems we fell in love:
a weary, languid, lifeless kind of love.
Wind was rising in the millet fields, it was the equinox
and yet in streets and on roofs, on shop signs and in lungs,
that milky dust just kept heaping up.

씻김굿
— 떠도는 원혼의 노래

편히 가라네 날더러 편히 가라네
꺾인 목 잘린 팔다리 끌고 안고
밤도 낮도 없는 저승길 천리 만리
편히 가라네 날더러 편히 가라네.

잠들라네 날더러 고이 잠들라네
보리밭 풀밭 모래밭에 엎드려
피멍든 두 눈 억겁년 뜨지 말고
잠들라네 날더러 고이 잠들라네.

잡으라네 갈가리 찢긴 이 손으로
피묻은 저 손 따뜻이 잡으라네
햇빛 밝게 빛나고 새들 지저귀는
바람 다스운 새 날 찾아왔으니
잡으라네 찢긴 이 손으로 잡으라네.

꺾인 목 잘린 팔다리로는 나는 못 가,
피멍든 두 눈 고이는 못 감아,
못 잡아, 이 찢긴 손으로는 못 잡아,
피묻은 저 손을 나는 못 잡아.

되돌아왔네, 피멍든 눈 부릅뜨고 되돌아왔네,
꺾인 목 잘린 팔다리 끌고 안고
하늘에 된서리 내리라 부드득 이빨 갈면서.

이 갈가리 찢긴 손으로는 못 잡아,
피묻은 저 손 나는 못 잡아,

Ssitkim Kut
A wandering spirit's song

Go in peace, they say, go in peace.
With broken neck, hugging severed limbs,
go a thousand, ten thousand *ri* to the land beyond,
without night or day; go in peace, they say, go in peace.

Sleep now, they say, sleep quietly now.
Though a myriad million years pass, never open those eyes
blinded with blood as you fell in barley field, meadow,
or patch of sand; sleep now, they say, sleep quietly now.

Seize hold, with your slashed and slivered hand
seize warmly hold of these blood-covered hands.
A new day has come, the sun is shining bright,
birds are caroling, the breeze is balmy,
so seize hold with your slivered hand, they say, seize hold.

I cannot go with my broken neck and severed limbs,
I cannot quietly close my blood-blinded eyes,
cannot seize hold, cannot seize with this slivered hand,
I cannot seize your blood-covered hands.

I have come back, blood-blinded eyes glaring, I have returned
with my broken neck, hugging severed limbs;
I grind my teeth and wish bitter frost may drop from heaven.

I cannot seize hold with this slivered hand,
I cannot seize your blood-covered hands;

골목길 장바닥 공장마당 도선장에
줄기찬 먹구름되어 되돌아왔네,
사나운 아우성되어 되돌아왔네.

*씻김굿 : 전라도 지방에서 많이 하는 굿으로, 원통한 넋을 위로해서 저
세상으로 편히 가게 하는 것이 목적임.

I have come back, a dense storm-cloud,
to alleys, markets, factories, quays;
I have come back, a violent clamor.

* The Ssitkim Kut is a ceremony often celebrated in the Cholla provinces, designed
to comfort unhappy spirits and convey them to a place of rest.

소리
— 떠도는 이의 노래

너는 나를 칼날 위에 서게 한다
너는 나를 불 앞에 서게 한다
너는 나를 물 속에 뛰어들게 한다

한밤에 길을 떠나게 한다
외로운 고장 썰렁한 장바닥에서
진종일 떨며 서성거리게 한다
귀먹은 땜쟁이 길동무삼아
산마을 갯마을을 떠돌게 한다

지는 해 등에 업고 긴 그림자로
꿈 속에서 고향을 찾게 한다
엿도가에서 옹기전에서 달비전에서
부사귀 몽달귀 동무되어 뛰게 한다
새벽에 눈뜨고 강물소리를 듣게 한다

너는 나를 불을 두려워하게 한다
물 속에 뛰어들기를 물리치게 한다
그래서 한밤에 다시 돌아오게 한다
골방에 깊이 숨어서 떨게 한다

그러나 너는 나를 되떠나게 한다
비틀대고 절뚝거리는 이들 데불고
버려진 포구에서 썩어가는 갯벌에서
마파람 하늬바람에 취하게 한다
너는 다시 나를 칼날 위에 서게 한다.

The Voice

A wanderer's song

You make me stand on a sword blade.
You make me stand by the fire.
You make me leap into streams.

You make me leave home late at night.
You make me loiter all day long
on the chill market places of lonely towns.
You make me wander from hill towns to coast
with some deaf and dumb tinker my sole companion.

The setting sun in my back, my shadow long,
you make me look for home in my dreams.
You make me go rushing with goblins and ghosts
from stalls selling taffy, pots, and hair.
You make me wake at daybreak to a river's roar.

You make me fear fire.
You make me refuse to plunge into streams.
And so you make me reach home at midnight.
You make me hide shuddering in secret store-rooms.

Then you make me leave home again.
You make me get drunk with south west winds
at abandoned harbors in stinking mud-flats,
in company with the halt and lame.
Once more you make me stand on a sword blade.

새벽
— 휴전선을 떠도는 혼령의 대화

보이나, 저 사람들이 보이나.
화해의 시대라고 야단들을 치는군.
배에 기름 끼면 간사한 꾀만 늘지.
죽도록 고생한 자들까지 왜 덩달아 맞북 치지.
늙고 지쳤으니까.
암, 늙고 지쳤으니까
우리도 이렇게 함께 앉았으니 이것이 화해인가.
서로 쏘고 찌른 상처 매만지며 함께 앉았으니까.
아닐세, 우린 서로 미워한 일 없지.
아닐세, 우린 옛날로 돌아가면 되지.
자 떠나세, 동이 트네.
자, 떠나세, 날선 낫 하나씩 들고.
자, 떠나세, 원수를 찾아서.

— 이른 새벽 휴전선 부근,
경지정리로 파헤쳐진 무덤 속에서
두개골들이 웅성거리는 소리를 듣는다.

Dawn

Spoken by spirits wandering along the armistice line

Did you see those people? Did you see?
Making such a fuss about an Age of Reconciliation?
The fatter they get, the more crafty their cunning.
Why do even they who suffered and died do the same?
Because they're old and weary.
Surely because they're old and weary.
We're squatting here together: is this reconciliation?
Squatting here together, caressing the wounds
     where we shot and stabbed each other.
It can't be: we never hated each other.
It can't be: we should go back to the good old days.
Off we go now, day is breaking.
Off we go now, each with his sharp sickle.
Off we go now, in search of the foe.

— At dawn, somewhere near the DMZ,
in a tomb plowed over after farmland readjustments,
two skeletons can be heard chattering together.

열림굿* 노래
— 휴전선을 떠도는 혼령의 노래 1

네 뼈는 바스라져 돌이 되고
네 팔다리 으깨어져 물이 되어
이루었구나 이 나라 한복판에
크고 깊은 산과 강 이루었구나

네 살은 썩어 흙이 되고
내 피 거름되어 흙 속에 배어
피웠구나 산기슭 강가에
붉고 노란 온갖 꽃 피웠구나

내가 쏜 괴로움에 네게 찔린 아픔에
아흔아홉 고비 황천길
되돌아오기 몇만 밤이던가
울고 떠돌기 몇만 날이던가

이제는 형제들 모여 붙안고 울 때
네 바스라진 머리통에 내 혀를 대고
내 깨어진 어깨에 네 입술을 대고
마음 활짝 열어제껴 통곡할 때

못나고 어리석었던 한세월을 우는구나
우리를 갈라놓고 등져 세우고
갈가리 찢은 자들 찾아 길 나서는구나
너를 쏜 총과 나를 찌른 칼을 버릴 때

우리 몸에 붙은 더러운 먼지를 털 때
원수들에게 더럽혀진 마음을 씻을 때

Yollim Kut Song

Sung by spirits wandering along the Armistice Line

Your bones have crumbled and turned into stones,
your limbs have been crushed and turned into water
and risen up now as vast mountains, deep rivers,
risen up in this country's heart.

Your flesh has rotted and turned into soil,
your blood has turned into compost enriching the soil
and blossomed now, all kinds of red and yellow flowers
have blossomed at mountain foot, along river banks.

How many thousand nights have we spent returning,
how many thousand days lamenting, wandering
on death's tawny path with its ninety-nine crests,
you with the pain I gave you, I tormented with pain by you?

Now is the time we meet, brethren together, embrace and weep,
when I strike my tongue against your shattered skull
and you apply your lips to my broken shoulders,
as we wail laments with open hearts.

We mourn the time when we were stupid, and crazy.
We set out in quest of those who slashed us to bits,
divided us, alienated us from one another.
As we cast aside the gun that shot, the knife that stabbed,

as we wipe away the sordid dust soiling our bodies,
wash the hearts defiled by our enemies;

이제는 울음을 멈추고 몸에 붙은
우리들 몸에 붙은 때와 얼룩을 씻을 때

서로 찌르고 쏜 형제들 다시
아픈 상처 어루만지며 통곡하는구나
썩어 문드러진 팔다리 쓸어안고 우는구나
크고 깊은 산과 강이 따라 우는구나

붉고 노란 온갖 꽃들이 우는구나
들판을 덮은 갈대들이 우는구나
그러나 지금은 우리들 길 나설 때
원수들 찾아 눈 부릅뜨고 우는구나

*열림굿 : 여주, 원성, 중원 지방의 정월놀이로, 지난 한 해의 다툼과
갈림을 씻는 화해 놀이. '열림'은 연다는 뜻과 풍요의 뜻 둘을 함께
가지고 있었으며, 굿을 무당이 주재하지 않고 마을 젊은이들이 자유로운
형식으로 하는 것이 특색임.

now, as we silence our laments and wash away
the dirt and stains that adhere to our flesh;

look: these brothers that once shot and stabbed one another,
now lament as they gently caress each other's sore wounds.
They weep, lightly embracing rotten crumbling limbs.
Vast mountains, deep rivers weep in accord.

All the red and yellow flowers are weeping too.
The reeds that cover the meadows weep.
But now, as we set out along the path
in quest of our foes, they are weeping with glaring eyes.

* The Yollim Kut is celebrated annually in the southwestern regions as a way of
putting an end to quarrels and disputes that have arisen in the village community
during the past year. It is celebrated by the younger villagers, without a shaman.

허재비굿*을 위하여
— 두 원혼의 주고받는 소리

잡아주오 내 손을 잡아주오.
흙 속에 묻힌 지 삼십 년
원통해서 썩지 못한 내 손을 잡아주오.
총알에 으깨어지고 칼날에 찢어진
내 팔다리를 일으켜주오.
밤마다 내 어머니 흐느껴 우는 소리 들리지만
나는 갈 수 없어,
산과 들을 헤매이며 나를 찾는
어머니 통곡소리 들리지만 나는 못 가.
철적은 비 구죽죽이 내리는 밤이면
머리 쥐어뜯으며 흐느끼기도 하고
늑대 애터지게 울어쌓는 찬 새벽이면
엉금엉금 흙 속을 기어보기도 하지만,
내 형제가 내 가슴을 쏜 것이
나는 원통해,
내 친구가 내 어깨 찌른 일을
나는 믿을 수가 없어.
복사꽃처럼 붉던 두 볼에 젖무덤에 허벅지에
검푸른 풀 돋으리라 어이 알았으리.
잡아주오 내 손을 잡아주오.
원통해서 썩지 못한 내 손을 잡아주오.

잡으리라 내 그대 손 잡으리라.
나 또한 어깨에 등허리에 머리통에
총알이 박힌 채 대창이 꽂힌 채.
우리가 쏘고 맞고 찌르고 찔리면서
죽던 그날을 나는 잊지 못해.

162

For a Hojaebi Kut

An exchange between two tormented ghosts

Take hold of my hand. Take hold.
Take hold of this hand, so full of bitter *han* it has not rotted
despite being buried for thirty years.
Restore my limbs, smashed by bullets
and slashed with swords.
I hear my mother's nightly sobbing
but I cannot go;
I hear mother's laments as she goes wandering
over hills and fields in search of me, but I cannot go.
On nights when unseasonable rain sluices down,
sobbing I tear at my hair;
in icy dawns when wolves howl wretchedly
I crawl under the ground
and grieve to think
how my brother shot me in the chest;
I cannot believe that my friend
stabbed me between the shoulders.
How could I guess that dark grass would grow
on my peach-blossom-pink cheeks, my swelling breasts,
my thighs?
Take hold of my hand. Take hold.
Take hold of this hand, so full of bitter *han* it has not rotted.

I will take hold of your hand. I will take hold.
I too was riddled with bullets, left full of wounds
in my back and waist and skull.
I cannot forget that day when we shot and hit home,

새빨간 노을 속으로
가마귀떼 날아가던 그 가을 언덕을
나는 잊지 못해.
피 쏟으며 쓰러지던 그대 그
붉은 입술을 나는 잊지 못해.
삼천 날 삼천 밤을 뉘우쳤지,
흙 속에서 통곡하며 뉘우쳤지.
우리는 원수가 아니라오, 미워하지도 않았다오.
잡으리라 내 그대 손 잡으리라.
원통해서 썩지 못한 그대 손 잡으리라.
아직 더운 내 입김으로 내 혓바닥으로
그대 상처 녹이리라.
그리하여 날아가리라 함께 날아가리라,
그대 어머니 내 어머니 울음소리 들리는 곳,
내 친구들 형제들 노랫소리 울음소리
가득한 곳으로.
잡으리라 원통해서 썩지 못한
그대 손 잡으리라.
햇빛 온 누리에 가득한 곳으로
그대 손 잡고 날아가리라.

*허재비굿 : 동해안 지방에서 젊은 원혼의 인연을 맺어줄 때 하는 굿으로,
화해의 뜻이 깊음.

stabbed and were stabbed, and died.
I cannot forget
that autumnal hill where the rooks were flying
home into the crimson sunset.
I cannot forget your crimson lips
as you fell there spouting blood.
Three thousand days, three thousand nights, I have repented;
singing laments beneath the ground, I have repented.
We are no enemies; we never hated one another.
I will take hold of your hand. I will take hold.
I will take hold of your hand,
so full of bitter *han* it has not rotted.
I will warm your wounds
with my still warm breath, and my tongue.
Then we will fly away, fly away together.
to where your mother and mine can be heard weeping,
to the places full
of the songs and laments of friends and brothers.
I will take hold of your hand,
so full of bitter *han* it has not rotted.
Holding your hand, I will fly away
to a place where the whole world is full of sunlight.

* *The Hojaebi Kut is a ritual celebrated in the eastern coastal regions for the rest of those who die young. It is particularly full of a sense of reconciliation.*

세월

흙 속을 헤엄치는
꿈을 꾸다가
자갈밭에 동댕이쳐지는
꿈을 꾸다가……

지하실 바닥 긁는
사슬소리를 듣다가
무덤 속 깊은 곳의
통곡소리를 듣다가……

창문에 어른대는
하얀 달을 보다가
하늘을 훨훨 나는
꿈을 꾸다가……

Time Passes

I dreamed
I was swimming through the ground
I dreamed
I was thrown into a stony field . . .

I heard chains
scraping across a cellar floor
I heard lamentations
from deep within a tomb . . .

I saw the pale moon
glimmering through a window
I dreamed
I was flying across the sky . . .

명매기 집

옛고장 사람들은 우리들더러
도망질쳤다 종주먹질하고
이 고장 사람들은 또
숨어들어왔다 눈흘긴다
저쪽에선 되돌아오지 말라 침 배앝고
이쪽에선 발 들여놓지 말라
금줄 쳐 막는다
달구지에 용달차에 화물차에 실려온
누더기라 헌 짐짝 서덜에 풀어놓고
산비알에 까맣게 움막을 치니
그래도 좋아라 갈갬질치는 내 새끼들아
이게 간데없이 명매기* 집이로구나
우리가 왜 모르겠느냐
너희 눈에 담긴 눈물이 머잖아
파랗게 불꽃으로 번득일 것을
활활 세상을 태우는
불꽃으로 타오를 것을

*명매기 : 여름 한철 개울가 바위 벼랑에 집을 짓고 사는 새. 불길한
새라 하여 사람들이 동네 안에 들어오는 것을 꺼리는데, 그 눈에서 파란
빛이 일면 큰 재앙이 온다는 얘기가 있음.

Rock Swift's Nest

Country folk in the old hometown used to
shake angry fists, accusing us of running off,
while the country folk hereabouts
glare fiercely, accusing us of sneaking in.
Get away and don't come back, those spat.
Never set foot here again!
These set up barricades.
On a stony hill field we unload tattered bundles
off a wagon, delivery van, truck,
build a grim mud hovel on some mountain slope.
"It's better than nothing, my little fledglings
can frolic here. It's like a rock swift's nest."
Ah, we know for sure:
those tears now brimming in your eyes will soon
flash out as green flames,
will soar up as flames
engulfing all the world.

* Rock swifts are a kind of bird that build their nests in blazing mid-summer high
on cliffs beside streams. They are associated with disasters and people dread to see
them around their houses. It is said that if a green light shines from their eyes it
presages some great misfortune.

가난한 사랑노래
— 이웃의 한 젊은이를 위하여

가난하다고 해서 외로움을 모르겠는가
너와 헤어져 돌아오는
눈 쌓인 골목길에 새파랗게 달빛이 쏟아지는데.
가난하다고 해서 두려움이 없겠는가
두 점을 치는 소리
방범대원의 호각소리 메밀묵 사려 소리에
눈을 뜨면 멀리 육중한 기계 굴러가는 소리.
가난하다고 해서 그리움을 버렸겠는가
어머님 보고 싶소 수없이 뇌어보지만
집 뒤 감나무에 까치밥으로 하나 남았을
새빨간 감 바람소리도 그려보지만.
가난하다고 해서 사랑을 모르겠는가
내 볼에 와 닿던 네 입술의 뜨거움
사랑한다고 사랑한다고 속삭이던 네 숨결
돌아서는 내 등뒤에 터지던 네 울음.
가난하다고 해서 왜 모르겠는가
가난하기 때문에 이것들을
이 모든 것들을 버려야 한다는 것을.

A Poor Love Song
— for a young neighbor

Why shouldn't you feel lonely, just because you're poor?
Leaving you, I make my way home
down a snowy alley drenched in pallid moonlight.
Why shouldn't you feel fear, just because you're poor?
Two strident sounds,
a night watchman's whistle and "Buckwheat paste!"
rouse me, with the distant roar of turning machines.
Why should you give up longing, just because you're poor?
You keep repeating: I want to see Mother;
you imagined the wind among red persimmons
left on the backyard tree for magpies to eat,
but why shouldn't you feel love, just because you're poor?
The warmth of your lips against my cheek,
your breath whispering I love you, I love you,
your outburst of tears behind me when I turned away.
Why shouldn't you know, just because you're poor?
Know that you're supposed to give up these things,
all these things, because you're poor.

갈구렁달

지금쯤 물거리 한 짐 해놓고
냇가에 앉아 저녁놀을 바라볼 시간⋯⋯
시골에서 내몰리고 서울에서도 떠밀려
벌판에 버려진 사람들에겐 옛날밖에 없다
지금쯤 아이들 신작로에 몰려
갈갬질치며 고추잠자리 잡을 시간⋯⋯

아무도 들어주지 않는 목소리로 외쳐대고
아무도 보아주지 않는 몸짓으로 발버둥치다
지친 다리 끄는 오르막에서 바라보면
너덜대는 지붕 위에 갈구렁달*이 걸렸구나
시들고 찌든 우리들의 얼굴이 걸렸구나

*갈구렁달 : 황해도, 충청도 바닷가에서 쪽박같이 쪼그라든 달을 말함.

Shrunken Moon

It's about now that we used to squat at the riverside
and watch the sunset after gathering sea vegetables . . .
driven away from the village, forced to leave Seoul, abandoned
in the plains, people like us have nothing but the old days.
It's about now that the kids clustered on the highway
used to be frolicking as they caught red dragonflies . . .

I shout out a cry that no one hears,
I squirm in a gesture that no one sees;
then from the hill that finishes my weary legs, look,
above the wavering roofs a shrunken moon is hanging!
A face just like ours, all withered and worn.

* "Shrunken moon" is an expression used in some coastal regions of north and
central Korea to describe the moon when it appears distorted.

두물머리
— 두물머리에서 만난 북한강과 남한강이 주고받는 노래

"조심조심 지뢰 사이를 지났지
긁히고 찢기면서 철조망도 넘었지
못다 운 넋들의 울음소리도 들었지
하얀 해골 덜 삭은 뼈에 대고
울면서 울면서 입맞춤도 하였지"

"내 몸에 밴 것은 눈물뿐이라네
쫓겨난 농투산이들 한숨뿐이라네
눈비 바람은 갈수록 맵차고
온 벌에 안개 더욱 짙어가지만
나는 보았네 땅 뚫고 솟는 빛살을
노래처럼 힘차고 굵은 빛살을"

"얼싸안아보자꾸나 어루만져보자꾸나
너는 북에서 나는 남에서
온갖 서러운 일 기막힌 짓 못된 꼴
다 겪으면서 예까지 흘러오지 않았느냐
내 살에 네 피를 섞고
네 뼈에 내 입김 불어넣으면
그 온갖 것 모두 빛이 되리니
춤추자꾸나 아침햇살에 몸 빛내면서"

A Song of Two Rivers

Sung at the confluence of the North and South Han rivers

"Ah, I slipped between land-mines, so cautiously;
I crossed tangled barbed wire that scratched and tore;
I heard the ceaseless weeping of grieving ghosts;
I caressed white skeletons and bones less scrubbed,
weeping, weeping, as I kissed them there."

"My whole body is full of nothing but tears;
nothing but the breath of peasants expelled from the land;
the sleet-filled wind grows ever more bitter,
the mist grows thicker across all the plain,
yet I have seen a glory bursting from the ground,
a substantial glory, and mighty as songs."

"Now let's embrace! Now let's caress!
For we each have flowed hither,
you from north, I from south,
enduring such sorrow, amazement, wretchedness.
Once your blood mingles with my flesh,
once my breath penetrates your bones,
all those things will be turned into light;
now let's dance, one body blazing in the rising sun."

* *The North and South branches of the Han River unite just east of Seoul.*

길

길을 가다가
눈발치는 산길을 가다가
눈 속에 맺힌 새빨간 열매를 본다
잃어버린 옛 얘기를 듣는다
어릴 적 멀리 날아가버린
노래를 듣는다

길을 가다가
갈대 서걱이는 강길을 가다가
빈 가지에 앉아 우는 하얀 새를 본다
헤어진 옛 친구를 본다
친구와 함께
잊혀진 꿈을 찾는다

길을 가다가
산길을 가다가
산길 강길 들길을 가다가
내 손에 가득 들린 빨간 열매를 본다
내 가슴 속에서 퍼덕이는 하얀 새
그 날개 소리를 듣는다

그것들과 어울어진 내
노래 소리를 듣는다
길을 가다가

The Road

Walking along a road,
walking along a snow-swept mountain road,
I see bright crimson berries growing in the snow.
I hear old tales long forgotten.
I hear songs
that flew far away in childhood times.

Walking along a road,
walking along a riverside road crunchy with reeds,
I see white birds perching to sing on bare branches.
I see long-lost old friends.
I rediscover dreams
forgotten together with those friends.

Walking along a road,
walking along a mountain road,
walking along mountain, river, meadow roads,
I see crimson berries filling my hands full.
I hear the beating wings
of the white bird fluttering in my breast.

I hear the sound of the song
I sing, united with all those things,
walking along the road.

오월은 내게

오월은 내게 사랑을 알게 했고
달뜨는 밤의 설레임을 알게 했다
뻐꾹새 소리의 기쁨을 알게 했고
돌아오는 길의 외로움에 익게 했다
다시 오월은 내게 두려움을 가르쳤다
저자거리를 메운 군화발소리 총칼소리에
산도 강도 숨죽여 웅크린 것을 보았고
붉은 피로 물든 보도 위에서
신조차 한숨을 쉬는 것을 보았다
마침내 오월에 나는 증오를 배웠다
불없는 지하실에 주검처럼 처박혀
일곱밤 일곱낮을 이를 가는 법을 배웠다
원수들의 이름 손바닥에 곱새기며
그 이름 위에 칼날을 꽂는 꿈을 익혔다
그리하여 오월에 나는 복수의 기쁨을 알았지만
찌른 만큼 찌르고 밟힐 만큼 밟는 기쁨을 배웠지만
오월은 내게 갈 길을 알게 했다
함께 어깨를 낄 동무들을 알게 했고
소리쳐 부를 노래를 알게 했다

May's Lessons

The month of May gave me knowledge of love,
of the sweet unrest at moon-rise.
It showed me the joy of a cuckoo's song
and how lonely the homebound traveler is.
Next the month of May gave me lessons in fear.
I saw hills and rivers hold their breath and cower
at the sound of army boots, guns and swords,
    filling every market alley.
I saw even God sigh
over sidewalks stained with crimson blood.
At last I learned hatred in the month of May.
Confined like a corpse in an unlit cellar,
I learned how to grind my teeth: seven nights, seven days.
Tracing enemies' names in the palm of my hand,
I practiced dreams where I stabbed those names with a knife.
So in the month of May, I learned the joys of revenge,
I learned the joy of stabbing as stabbed,
    of trampling as trampled,
then the month of May showed me the way to go.
It showed me companions to join with, arm in arm,
and it taught me songs to bellow out.

가난한 북한 어린이
— 지도*에서

엄마는 돈 벌러 서울 가서 이태째 소식 없고
아빠도 엄마 찾아 집 나간 지 여러 달포
이제 보름만 더 있다 온다는
어쩌다 전화로 듣는 아빠 목소리는 늘 취해 있다
두 동생 아침밥 먹여 학교 보내고
열두살 난 언니 하루 안 거르고 정거장에 나와 서지만
진종일 서울 땅장수만 차를 오르내리고
다 저녁때 지쳐 돌아오면
저희들끼리 끓여 먹은 라면 냄비 팽개쳐둔 채
두 동생 텔레비전 만화에 넋을 잃었다
다시 밥 대신 라면으로 저녁을 끓이고
열두살 난 언니는 일기에 쓴다 전화도
텔레비전도 없는 북한 어린이들이 가엾다고
가난한 북한 어린이들이 불쌍하다고
엄마 아빠 돈 벌어 돌아올 날을 믿으면서

*지도 : 신안의 어촌으로 옛날에는 섬이었으나 지금은 다리로 육지와
연결돼 있음.

Poor North Korean Kids
— overheard in Ji-do Island

Ma went to Seoul to earn money, no news for two years now;
it's been several months since Dad left home to look for her;
sometimes he phones, he'll be back in another fortnight;
his voice always sounds as though he's drunk.
The eldest, a girl eleven years old, feeds the two others,
sends them off to school; then every day without fail
goes to stand at the bus-stop but all day long the only people
getting on and off the bus are estate agents from Seoul;
then when she comes home exhausted in the evening,
the two young ones are absorbed in cartoons on the television,
the pan where they boiled up *ramyon* left lying unwashed.
The eleven-year-old boils *ramyon* for supper instead of rice,
then writes in her diary she feels so sorry
for poor North Korean kids with no telephone, no television;
how pitiful poor North Korean kids are. Always feeling sure
one day Ma and Dad will come home with their earnings.

* *Ji-do is the name of a small island off the south coast of Korea.*

그림

옛사람의 그림 속으로
들어가고 싶은 때가 있다
배낭을 멘 채 시적시적
걸어들어가고 싶은 때가 있다
주막집도 들어가보고
색시들 수놓는 골방문도 열어보고
대장간에서 풀무질도 해보고
그러다가 아예 나오는 길을
잃어버리면 어떨까
옛사람의 그림 속에
갇혀버리면 어떨까
문득 깨달을 때가 있다
내가 오늘의 그림 속에
갇혀 있다는 것을
나가는 길을 잃어버렸다는 것을
두드려도 발버둥쳐도
문도 길도
찾을 수 없다는 것을
오늘의 그림에서
빠져나가고 싶을 때가 있다
배낭을 메고 밤차에 앉아
지구 밖으로 훌쩍
떨어져나가고 싶을 때가 있다

Paintings

There are times when I long to become part
of an old-time painting.
There are times when I long to go trudging in,
with my knapsack on,
to enter a tavern,
to push open a back-room door where lasses sit embroidering,
to work the bellows in a blacksmith's shop;
just suppose I couldn't find
the way back out, what then?
Suppose I were trapped
in an old-time painting, what then?
There are times when I suddenly realize
that I'm trapped
inside a modern-day painting,
and can't find the way out of it,
knock and struggle though I may,
I just can't find
any door or exit.
There are times when I long to get out
of this modern-day painting.
There are times when I long to be sitting
in a night express, with my knapsack on,
on my way right out of this world.

여름날

— 마천*에서

버스에 앉아 잠시 조는 사이
소나기 한줄기 지났나보다
차가 갑자기 분 물이 무서워
머뭇거리는 동구 앞
허연 허벅지를 내놓은 젊은 아낙
철벙대며 물을 건너고
산뜻하게 머리를 감은 버드나무가
비릿한 살냄새를 풍기고 있다

*마천 : 경남 산청군에 속하는 지리산 아랫마을.

A Summer's Day
— in Mach'on

We must have gone through a shower
while I dozed off sitting in the bus.
The vehicle lingers at a village entrance
intimidated by the sudden spread of water
as a young woman wades splashing through the water
revealing pure white thighs
and a willow with freshly washed tresses
emits a faint odor of flesh.

* Mach'on is a village at the foot of Chiri Mountain in Sanch'ong County, South
Kyongsang Province.

나무 1
― 지리산에서

나무를 길러본 사람만이 안다
반듯하게 잘 자란 나무는
제대로 열매를 맺지 못한다는 것을
너무 잘나고 큰 나무는
제 치레하느라 오히려
좋은 열매를 갖지 못한다는 것을
한 군데쯤 부러졌거나 가지를 친 나무에
또는 못나고 볼품없이 자란 나무에
보다 실하고
단단한 열매가 맺힌다는 것을

나무를 길러본 사람만이 안다
우쭐대며 웃자란 나무는
이웃 나무가 자라는 것을 가로막는다는 것을
햇빛과 바람을 독차지해서
동무 나무가 꽃 피고 열매 맺는 것을
훼방한다는 것을
그래서 뽑거나
베어버릴 수밖에 없다는 것을
사람이 사는 일이 어찌 꼭 이와 같을까만

A Tree 1
— in Chiri Mountain

Only people who have grown trees know
that flawlessly grown trees
are utterly incapable of bearing fruit,
that finely grown, tall trees
are so busy looking good that as a rule
they are unable to produce good fruit,
while trees broken somewhere, or lacking a branch,
trees disfigured, nothing to look at,
yield healthy fruit
in plenty.

Only people who have grown trees know
that proud lofty trees
prevent surrounding trees from growing properly,
that by monopolizing sunlight and breeze
they hinder their fellow trees
from bearing flowers and fruit;
so they get cut down,
there's no other way than to root them out.
It may not be the same in human existence . . .

* *Chiri Mountain (Chiri-san) is a mountain range in the southern part of Korea.*

길

사람들은 자기들이 길을 만든 줄 알지만
길은 순순히 사람들의 뜻을 좇지는 않는다
사람을 끌고 가다가 문득
벼랑 앞에 세워 낭패시키는가 하면
큰물에 우정 제 허리를 동강내어
사람이 부득이 저를 버리게 만들기도 한다
사람들은 이것이 다 사람이 만든 길이
거꾸로 사람들한테 세상 사는
슬기를 가르치는 거라고 말한다
길이 사람을 밖으로 불러내어
온갖 곳 온갖 사람살이를 구경시키는 것도
세상 사는 이치를 가르치기 위해서라고 말한다
그래서 길의 뜻이 거기 있는 줄로만 알지
길이 사람을 밖에서 안으로 끌고 들어가
스스로를 깊이 들여다보게 한다는 것은 모른다
길이 밖으로가 아니라 안으로 나 있다는 것을
아는 사람에게만 길은 고분고분해서
꽃으로 제 몸을 수놓아 향기를 더하기도 하고
그늘을 드리워 사람들이 땀을 식히게도 한다
그것을 알고 나서야 사람들은 비로소
자기들이 길을 만들었다고 말하지 않는다

The Path

People believe that they create a path for themselves but
the path does not quietly conform to what they intend.
Either it drags them onward until suddenly
there they are, stranded in failure at the edge of a cliff,
or it deliberately dives into a flood, forcing them to leave it.
Seeing this, people claim that the man-made path teaches
the wisdom of living, not the other way round;
equally they claim that it calls people abroad
and shows them every kind of place and way of living;
that is how it instructs them in the principles of life.
So they believe that such is all the path's intent.
They do not realize that the path leads people
from the outside inward
and obliges them to scrutinize their own hidden depths.
The path only grows subservient to those who know
that it leads not outward but inward,
embroidering itself with flowers, increasing their scent,
casting a shadow and enabling people to cool their sweat.
People who once know that will never be heard to claim
that it was they who made the path they took.

장미와 더불어

땅속에서 풀려난 요정들이
물오른 덩굴을 타고
쏜살같이 하늘로 달려 올라간다
다람쥐처럼 까맣게 올라가
문득 발 밑을 내려다보고는
어지러워 눈을 감았다
이내 다시 뜨면 아
저 황홀한 땅 위의 아름다움

너희들 더 올라가지 않고
대롱대롱 가지 끝에 매달려
꽃이 된들 누가 탓하랴
땅속의 말 하늘 높은 데까지
전하지 못한들 누가 나무라랴
발을 구르며 안달을 하던 별들
새벽이면 한달음에 내려오고
맑은 이슬 속에 스스로를 사위는
긴 입맞춤이 있을 터인데

With a Rose

Freed from underground, fairy spirits
ride up sap-filled vines,
then speed heavenward like arrows.
Shooting upward, as far above as the squirrels,
suddenly they look below their feet
and shut their eyes, seized with vertigo.
Opening them again an instant after: Ah!
The beauty of the enraptured earth seen from above

while you rise no farther
but hang dangling at the tips of branches;
whose fault is it if you turned into flowers?
Who should blame you if you failed to convey the words
of the ultimate underground to highest heaven?
The stars that impatiently kicked their feet
will drop down in a flash at break of day
and in clear dewdrops consume themselves
in long protracted kisses.

겨울 숲

굴참나무 허리에 반쯤 박히기도 하고
물푸레나무를 떠받치기도 하면서
엎드려 있는 나무가 아니면
겨울숲은 얼마나 싱거울까
산짐승들이나 나무꾼들 발에 채여
이리저리 나뒹굴다가
묵밭에 가서 처박힌 돌멩이들이 아니면
또 겨울숲은 얼마나 쓸쓸할까
나뭇가지에 걸린 하얀 낮달도
낮달이 들려주는 얘기와 노래도
한없이 시시하고 맥없을 게다
골짜기 낮은 곳 구석진 곳만을 찾아
잦아들듯 흐르는 실개천이 아니면
겨울숲은 얼마나 메마를까
바위틈에 돌틈에 언덕배기에
모진 바람 온몸으로 맞받으며
눕고 일어서며 버티는 마른풀이 아니면
또 겨울숲은 얼마나 허전할까

Winter Woodlands

If it weren't for the fallen tree
half piercing an oak tree's trunk
and propping up an ash tree,
how very tedious the winter woodlands would be.
If it weren't for the pebbles kicked by the feet
of beasts or of woodcutters,
rolling hither and thither
and finally embedded in the little plot cleared on the slope
how very dreary the winter woodlands would be.
The white daylight moon dangling in the branches,
the songs and tales, too, of the daylight moon,
would all be infinitely dreary and dull.
If it weren't for the trickle of water ever flowing, dropping
as if seeking the inmost recess of the valley's lowest point,
how very thirsty the winter woodlands would be.
If it weren't for the dry grass bending, rising, firmly resisting,
taking head-on the bitter blasts of the wind
between rocks and stones and on hilltops,
how very empty the winter woodlands would be.

담장 밖

번듯한 나무 잘난 꽃들은 다들 정원에 들어가 서고
억센 풀과 자잘한 꽃마리만 깔린 담장 밖 돌밭
구멍가게에서 소주병 들고 와 앉아보니 이곳이
내가 서른에 더 몇해 빠대고 다닌 바로 그곳이다.
허망할 것 없어 서러울 것은 더욱 없어
땀에 젖은 양말 벗어 널고 윗도리 베고 누우니
보이누나 하늘에 허옇게 버려진 빛 바랜 별들이
희미하게 들판에 찍힌 우리들 어지러운 발자국 너머.
가죽나무에 엉기는 새소리 어찌 콧노래로 받으랴
굽은 나무 시든 꽃들만 깔린 담장 밖 돌밭에서
어느새 나도 버려진 별과 꿈에 섞여 누워 있는데.

Outside the Wall

Splendid trees, magnificent flowers, grow inside the garden,
while there is nothing but tough grass and tiny flowers
in the stony ground stretching outside the wall,
where I sit with a bottle of *soju* from the tiny store, here,
where I have been laboring for thirty years past and more.
With no need to feel futile and even less call to be sorrowful,
spreading my wet socks on the wall to dry,
reclining with my head pillowed on my jacket,
I can see pale stars abandoned faint in the sky above
beyond our footsteps dimly printed across the fields.
How can I idly hum to the birdsong
       creeping from the ailanthus?
In the stony ground stretching outside the wall
with bent trees and shriveled flowers,
I lie mingled with abandoned stars and dreams.

낙일 (落日)

새말갛게 떠오를 때는 기쁨이 되고
뜨겁게 담금질할 때는 힘이 되었지
구름에 가렸을 때는 그리움이 되고
천둥 번개에 밀릴 때는 안타까움이 되었지
비바람에 후줄근하게 젖어 처지기도 하고
어쩌다가는 흉하게 일그러지기도 했지만
드디어 새맑음도 뜨거움도 홀연히 잊고
그리움도 안타까움도 훌훌 떨쳐버리고
표표히 서산을 넘는 황홀한 아름다움

말하지 말자 거기서 새로 꿈이 싹튼다고는

Sunset

Source of joy when rising clear
and source of might when tempering with heat,
then source of yearning when hidden by clouds
and source of regret when banished by thunder storms.
Sometimes hanging limply drenched after a storm of rain,
occasionally even contorted and ugly,
then suddenly forgetting all clarity and heat,
yearning and regret quite sloughed away,
ecstatic beauty carelessly dropping into the west.

Let it not be said that there dreams come budding fresh.

Lee Si-Young
이 시영

Born in Kurye, South Cholla Province, in 1949, Lee Si-Young (Lee Shi-Yŏng) began publishing poetry in 1969 and has so far produced eight volumes, beginning with his first volume 만월 *Manwo l* (*Full moon*) in 1976. Ten years passed before a second, 바람 속 으로 *Param sokŭro* (*Into the wind*) was published in 1986. Since then he has published regularly, with 길은 멀다 친구 여 *Ki rŭn mŏlda ch'inguyŏ* (*It's a long way, friend*, 1988), 이슬 맺힌 노래 *Isŭl maech'in norae* (*Songs soaked in dew*, 1991), 무늬 *Munŭi* (*Pattern*, 1994). In 1996, he published 사이 *Sai* (*Relationship*) and in 1997 조용한 푸른 하늘 *Choyonghan p'urŭn hanŭl* (*Quiet blue sky*). He served as vice-president of 창작과 비평사 *Ch'angjak kwa pip'yŏng* Publishing Company for a number of years.

The poem "One Snowy Evening" was first published in *Stand Magazine* (Winter 1997).

바람아

바람아 너희 나라엔 누가 있는가
날 저물면 산에서 내려와 문고리 두드리는
커다란 그림자가 있는가
뒷문 열고 기침하는 늙으신 어머니가 있는가
밤새도록 대밭에서 끄덕이다
땅 끝으로 사라지는 반딧불이 있는가
아버지가 있는가
바람아 너희 나라엔 얼굴도 없는가
서서 멈출 발자욱도 없는가
풀섶을 헤쳐가는 소리죽인 눈도 없는가
떨리는 가슴 닿을 다음 땅은 없는가
바람아 너희 나라엔 아무도 아무도 없는가

Tell Me, Wind

Tell me, wind, who is in your land?
Are there vast shadows
that come down at sunset and rattle the door latch?
Are there aged mothers who open the back door and cough?
Is there a glow of fireflies bobbing all night in bamboo groves
then fleeing away to the ends of the earth?
Are there fathers there?
Tell me, wind, are there no faces in your land?
Are there not even footprints poised motionless?
Are there no silent eyes piercing the undergrowth?
Is there no future land a trembling heart can reach?
Tell me, wind, is there no one, no one in your land?

너

불러다오
밤이 깊다
벌레들이 밤이슬에 뒤척이며
하나의 별을 애타게 부르듯이
새들이 마지막 남은 가지에 앉아
위태로이 나무를 부르듯이
그렇게 나를 불러다오
부르는 곳을 찾아
모르는 너를 찾아
밤 벌판에 떨면서
날 밝기 전에
나는 무엇이 되어 서고 싶구나
나 아닌 다른 무엇이 되어
걷고 싶구나
처음으로 가는 길을
끝없는 길을

You

Call my name.
It's late at night.
I want you to call out my name
just as insects call anxiously to stars,
as they toss and turn in the evening dew,
or as birds call out perilously to trees,
perched on the last remaining branch.
Oh, I long to be transformed, to stand there,
having found the place the call came from
and you, the unknown caller,
trembling in the plain by night
before day begins to break.
I long to walk
along a road I never took before,
along an endless road,
transformed into something other than I.

이름

밤이 깊어갈수록
우리는 누군가를 불러야 한다
우리가 그 이름을 부르지 않았을 때
잠시라도 잊었을 때
채쩍 아래서 우리를 부르는 뜨거운 소리를 듣는다

이 밤이 길어갈수록
우리는 누구에겐가로 가야 한다
우리가 가기를 멈췄을 때
혹은 가기를 포기했을 때
칼자욱을 딛고서 오는 그이의
아픈 발소리를 듣는다

우리는 누구인가를 불러야 한다
우리는 누구에겐가로 가야 한다
대낮의 숨통을 조이는 것이
형제의 찬 손일지라도
언젠가는 피가 돌아
고향의 논둑을 더듬는 다순 낮이 될지라도
오늘 조인 목을 뽑아
우리는 그에게로 가야만 한다
그의 이름을 불러야 한다
부르다가 쓰러져 그의 돌이 되기 위해
가다가 멈춰 서서 그의 장승이 되기 위해

A Name

As night grows darker
we have to call out someone's name.
If we should fail to call that person's name,
if we should forget, for even a moment,
we hear a burning voice calling us from under the whip.

As this night grows longer
we have to set out toward someone.
If we pause as we go or refuse to go,
we hear that person's painful steps
advancing toward us,
treading on knife blades.

We have to call out to someone.
We have to go toward someone.
We have to go toward that person,
stretching necks that were strangled today,
even if it's a brother's icy hand
that strangles the breathing of noon,
even though the blood returning some day become
a warm sickle tracing the edge of home village rice-fields.
We are forced to call that person's name,
to call, then fall, become that person's stone.
To go, then stop, and become that person's guardian pole.

* Guardian pole: pillars of wood or stone carved with human faces, traditionally
placed at the entrance to a village to ward off harmful influences.

사람들의 마을 Ⅰ

모르는 곳 모르는 고장 서성이다
돌아와 산도 보고
고향 강에 소리없이 와 닿는
등불도 보게 되는가
떠나는 이의 가슴도 강과 함께 머물렀다
먼 곳으로 떠나는 것이지만,
강과 함께 흐르고 흘렀다가
이제는 목 말라 돌아오는 이 맞아
목 축여주기 위해
바닥 깊이 등불을 켜는 마음으로
저 산도 지키며 산과 함께 가난하게 엎드린 사람들
저녁 끼니가 떨어지면 억새 같은 손등으로
밤이슬 젖혀 산을 캐고
새벽 밭에 나가 감자를 캐는
사람들의 마을을 나는 안다

여기에서 태어나고 자라 마을을 버리고 떠났던 사람들
혹은 백발이 되어, 혹은 팔 병신이 되어,
혹은 눈멀고 귀멀어,
혹은 쫓겨서, 혹은 배고파 돌아오는 이들
모두 한 팔로 안고
다른 팔로 쓰다듬어
강을 주고
산의 마음을 주는
가슴 두근거리는 이들의 마을을 나는 안다
서울서 기차를 타고 일곱 시간,
하늘 가까이 내려오다 강기슭에 멈춘 마을을

A Village of People   1

After lingering in an unknown place, an unknown location,
returning again, we view the hills.
Can't we see the lamp
silently touching the hometown river?
The hearts of those leaving still stay with the river.
They may be leaving for some distant place,
yet they flow and flow on with the river until it greets them
as they return in thirst and moisten their throats
by the heart kindling a lamp in its inmost recess
at the sight of those hills, the people prostrate in poverty
together with the hills, digging at the hills
with eulalia-wood hands moist with the dew
when there's nothing for supper, going out at dawn
to the fields and digging for potatoes.
I know a village of people who live like that.

People born and bred here, then left the village,
but at last they came back
gray-haired, or having lost the use of an arm, blind or deaf,
hunted or hungry; I know a village of such people
with hearts throbbing wildly,
embracing with one arm
caressing with the other,
giving the mountain's heart,
giving the river.
A village seven hours' train ride from Seoul
perched on a river bank, the sky inclining close.

사람들의 마을 Ⅱ

내 이대로는 마을로 들어설 수 없구나
기차를 타고 밤길을 걸어
새벽 강을 가까스로 건넜지만
찢긴 마음 부은 눈으로는
차마 어머니의 등불 부를 수 없구나
싸움에 지치면 언제든지 돌아와
목소리 낮춰 부르라고
밤새도록 이슬 속에 켜둔 등불
그러나 이 목마른 입술로는
답답한 가슴으로는 다가설 수 없구나
대밭 속에 서성이며 울먹이는 불빛 바라보다
날 밝기 전에 부끄런 발길 돌려
강을 건너야지 더 먼 곳으로 가는
기차를 타야지
가서 새 힘으로 돌같이 뭉쳐야지
이대로는, 이 떨리는 빈 주먹을 쥐고는
어머니를 찾을 수 없구나

A Village of People   2

I cannot possibly enter the village like this!
I took the train, walked down night paths
managed to cross the river at dawn,
but with a broken heart and swollen eyes
why, I don't have the heart to call out to mother's lamp!
Her lamp shines all night long in the dew,
saying: Come home any time when you're weary of fighting.
Lower your voice and call out.
But I can't possibly approach
with these parched lips, this anxious heart. Loitering
in the bamboo grove I gaze toward the lamp, almost in tears.
Before day breaks I must beat a shameful retreat
back across the river. I must catch a train
to somewhere farther away.
I must take fresh vigor, grow more solid like a stone.
I cannot possibly visit mother like this,
clenching trembling empty fists.

사람들의 마을 Ⅲ

어머니는 무슨 말씀 하시려는가 봅니다
앞가슴 다급히 감추고
새벽차로 올라오시어
아들 이름 불러놓고
어머니는 무슨 말씀 하시려는가 봅니다
한 손으로 물러앉으며
한 손으로 허공 저으며
어머니는 차마 무슨 말씀 하시려는가 봅니다.

A Village of People   3

Mother seems about to say something.
Urgently veiling her breast,
she came up on the night train
and called out her son's name;
now Mother seems about to say something,
holding herself back with one hand,
slashing the air with one hand.
Surely Mother seems about to say something.

정님이

용산역전 늦은 밤거리
내 팔을 끌다 화들짝 손을 놓고 사라진 여인
운동회 때마다 동네 대항 릴레이에서 늘 일등을 하여 밥솥을 타던
정님이누나가 아닐는지 몰라
이마의 흉터를 가린 긴 머리, 날랜 발
학교도 못다녔으면서
운동회 때만 되면 나보다 더 좋아라 좋아라
머슴 만득이 지게에서 점심을 빼앗아 이고 달려오던 누나
수수밭을 매다가도 새를 보다가도 나만 보면
흙묻은 손으로 달려와 청색 책보를
단단히 동여매 주던 소녀
콩깍지를 털어주며 맛있니 맛있니
하늘을 보고 웃던 하이얀 목
아버지도 없고 어머니도 없지만
슬프지 않다고 잡았던 메뚜기를 날리며 말했다
어느해 봄엔 높은 산으로 나물 캐러 갔다가
산뱀에 허벅지를 물려 이웃 처녀들에게 업혀와서도
머리맡으로 내 손을 찾아 산다래를 쥐여주더니
왜 가버렸는지 몰라
목화를 따고 물레를 잣고
여름밤이 오면 하얀 무릎 위에
정성껏 삼을 삼더니
동지섣달 긴긴 밤 베틀에 고개 숙여
달그당잘그당 무명을 잘도 짜더니
왜 바람처럼 가버렸는지 몰라
빈 정지 문 열면 서글서글한 눈망울로
이내 달려나올 것만 같더니

Chong-im

Late evening, in front of Yongsan station.
I think that girl who tugged my arm, then abruptly let go
and vanished, was perhaps Chong-im, who used to come first
in the relay race and win a rice-pot at every sports festival.
Long hair covering the scar on her brow, swift feet,
she couldn't attend school but when sports-day came
she was excited, more excited than I was.
She'd take the lunch from Manduk the laborer's back-frame,
put it on her head, and come running to me with it.
As she weeded the sorghum field or chased away the birds,
if she caught sight of me
she would dash up with muddy hands and firmly tie
the blue cloth bundle holding my books.
Shelling peas, she asked: Aren't they good? Aren't they good?
Her throat shone white as she looked heavenward and laughed.
She had no parents but said she wasn't sad,
freeing the grasshoppers she had caught.
One spring, she climbed high in the hills to gather fresh shoots,
and got bitten on the thigh by a snake. The neighborhood girls
brought her down on their backs, but she wanted my hand
about her pillow, gave me wild berries.
I wonder why she went away?
She'd pick cotton and spin it, spin flax on summer nights
to her heart's content, then in the long winter evenings hunch
over her loom, weave fine cotton cloth with a *crash* and a *thud*.
I wonder why she vanished like the wind?
I used to feel that I had only to open the empty kitchen door
and she would come hurrying out with her kindly eyes;

한번 가 왜 다시 오지 않았는지 몰라
식모 산다는 소문도 들렸고
방직공장에 취직했다는 말도 들렸고
영등포 색시집에서 누나를 보았다는 사람도 있었지만
어머니는 끝내 대답이 없었다
용산역전 밤 열한시 반
통금에 쫓기던 내 팔 붙잡다
날랜 발, 밤거리로 사라진 여인

I wonder why she left and never returned?
A rumor went round she was a housemaid somewhere,
report went about she had job in a textile factory,
someone said they'd seen her in a Yŏngdŭngp'o whorehouse,
but mother never uttered a word in reply.
That girl who grabbed my arm in front of Yongsan station
at eleven thirty last night, as I hurried to avoid the curfew,
then vanished down a dark alley with rapid steps: that girl . . .

* *The square in front of Seoul's Yongsan Station has long been well-known for its prostitutes, who used to be mostly girls come up from the rural villages to try to earn a living in Seoul.*

여름 속에서

귀가 트였으면
이 여름에는 두 귀가 트여
곧은 소리 들을 수 있었으면
밤하늘 변방에 뜬
의로운 소리 놓치지 말았으면
소리개 높이 날아
소리란 소리 다 파먹어도
벼랑에 가 우뢰처럼 부서지는 소리떼
한 마디도 놓치지 말았으면
묵은 귀 잘라버리고
햇볕에 잘 울리고
빗속에서 성성한
귀가 돋았으면

눈이 트였으면
두 눈 맑게 트여
十里를 볼 수 있었으면
十理 앞을 걷다가 전수된 사람들
풀밭에 떨어진 번개 같은 눈들 지나치지 말았으면
별 하나이 흘리는 눈물
아득한 땅에서 이는 연기
칼빛 속에서 소리치는 크나큰 손들
덥석 잡을 수 있었으면
썩은 눈 빼어버리고
나뭇잎에 닿으면 고요히 오므리고
쇠를 보면 한 자는 뛰쳐나올
커다란 눈을 가졌으면

In Summer

If only my ears would open.
If only this summer, with both ears open,
I could hear honest sounds.
If only I did not ignore the just sounds
rising at the edge of the evening sky.
Kites may fly high
and devour all those sounds
but if only I did not ignore a single one
of the host of sounds smashing like thunder against the cliff,
if only I could cut off my old ears
and sprout new ones
ringing clear in the sunlight,
fresh in the rain,

if only my eyes would open,
if only I could open both eyes clearly
and see for miles around,
if only I did not ignore the people who walked for miles before
being beheaded,
if only I did not pass by eyes like thunderbolts falling in fields
if only I could seize the tears that flow from every star,
the smoke that rises from distant lands,
those enormous hands screaming in the flashing of knives,
if only I could pluck out my rotten eyes
and gain enormous eyes
that would quietly pucker at the touch of a leaf
and pop out at the sight of iron . . .

눈이 내린다

아무도 살지 않는 나라에
눈이 내린다.
알지 못할 한 마디 맹세가
시퍼렇게 떨다가 스러지고
그 소리를 듣지 못한 소리가
그 위에 몸 비비며 스러지고
그 소리를 지키지 못한 소리가
소리 뒤에 쌓인다.

누구도 들을 수 없는 나라에
소리가 내린다.
소리 뒤에 주먹처럼 고요히 내린다.

아무것도 볼 수 없는 나라에
누구의 멍든 눈이 눈을 찾는다.
그 눈을 보지 못한 눈이 반짝이고
눈 뒤에서 반짝이던 눈이
자기의 없는 눈을 찾아
캄캄한 곳으로 사라진다.

아무도 찾을 수 없는 나라에
누구의 손이 묶여간다.
그 손을 잡는 손이 떨다가
자기 손을 잃어버린다.
잃어버린 자들의 가슴에 뭉클한
손이 내린다.

Snow is Falling

Snow is falling
in a land where no one lives.
One word, a pledge, doomed to be for ever unknown,
trembles livid and collapses.
A cry unable to hear that cry collapses on it, rubbing itself,
while cries unable to protect that cry
pile up behind the cries.

Cries are falling
in a land where no one can hear.
Falling quietly like fists behind those cries.

Someone's black eyes are seeking eyes
in a land where nothing can be seen.
Eyes sparkle, that cannot see those eyes,
and the eyes that once sparkled behind the eyes
in search of the eyes they lacked
vanish into the dark.

Someone's hands are led off in fetters
in a land that no one can find.
The hands holding those hands tremble
then loose their own hands.
In the hearts of those who have lost them
fleshy hands are falling.

기러기떼

기러기들 날아오른다
얼어붙은 찬 하늘 속으로 소리도 없이
싸움의 땅에서
초연이 걷히지 않는 땅에서
한 마리 두 마리 세 마리 네 마리
바람 속에서 오늘 눈감은 나의 형제들처럼

A Flock of Wild Geese

Wild geese fly on.
Into the frozen sky, soundlessly,
away from the land of fighting,
away from the land where gun-smoke never clears,
one bird, two birds, three birds, four birds,
like my brothers who today closed their eyes in the wind.

정적

반포대교를 건너면 그곳은 나타난다
아침마다 헬기가 내리고 뜨는
거대한 그린 필드
서남으론 삼각지에서 서빙고역,
동남으론 이태원에서 한남동,
북으론 남산 아래턱 남영동 후암동까지.
옛날엔 이 땅이 조선군 사령부였지
버스를 타고 가다 보면
수지 미용실, 크라운 골프샵, 킴스 드라이크리닝 건너편으로
숨죽인 듯 그저 고요한 막사들
1900년대엔 흰옷 입은 농꾼들이
곡괭이를 울러메고 와
내 땅 내놓아라 소리치다 피 흘리던 곳
그때의 감나무도 땀 배인 호박 구덩이도
해방의 길을 단숨에 달려온 지까다비도
철조망 안에서 썩고 있는데
오늘은 자작나무 흰 숲 아래로
유우에스 아미 용산 메인 포스트의
번쩍이는 선명한 금빛 마크, 햇빛 아래
굳게 닫힌 푸른색 문
그렇다 친구여, 오늘의 발자국은 소리가 없다
혈맹도, 미소짓는 흰 이빨의 굳은 악수도
저 낮은 퀀셋 그림자처럼
우리를 한번 삼키면 다시는 내놓으려 하지 않을 뿐
모습없이 소리없이 고요하기만 한
서남동북 수만 평 넓고 푸른 땅

Silence

If you cross Seoul's Panp'o Bridge you reach the spot:
a vast green field where choppers take off and land
from early morning, extending to the south west
from Samgakji to Sobinggo station
to the south east from Itaewon to Hannam-dong northwards
from Namyong-dong below Namsan as far as Huam-dong.
In old days this was the Choson Army's HQ, of course.
Now take a bus, go and look: across from
Suzie beauty parlor, Crown Golf-shop, Kim's Dry-cleaning,
you see barracks so quiet they seem to be holding their breath.
In the early 1900s simple farmers dressed in white
came to this spot waving hoes in threat,
shouted "Let go of my land!" and shed their blood.
The persimmon trees of old days, sweat-soaked pumpkin beds,
the sneakers that came rushing down the road of liberation,
are all rotting now inside the barbed wire fence
and today, below the grove of white birch trees, you see
the US Army Yongsan Main Post's clear golden emblem
in the sunlight, firmly closed green gates.
And friend, today's footsteps make no noise.
Alliances are sealed in blood, firm handshakes
with flashing white teeth, like the shadows of those squat huts.
If they succeed in making us theirs, they'll never let go again.
Devoid of shape, devoid of sound, simply silent there,
to north and south, east and west, that vast expanse of green.

어머니

어머니
이 높고 높은 아파트 꼭대기에서
조심조심 살아가시는 당신을 보면
슬픈 생각이 듭니다
죽어도 이곳으론 이사 오지 않겠다고
봉천동 산마루에서 버티시던 게 벌써 삼년 전인가요?
덜컥거리며 사람을 실어 나르는 엘리베이터에
아직도 더럭 겁이 나지만
안경 쓴 아들 내외가 다급히 출근하고 나면
아침마다 손주년 유치원길을 손목 잡고 바래다주는 것이
당신의 유일한 하루 일거리
파출부가 와서 청소하고 빨래해주고 가고
요구르트 아줌마가 외치고 가고
계단청소 하는 아줌마가 탁탁 쓸고 가버리면
무덤처럼 고요한 14층 7호
당신은 창을 열고 숨을 쉬어보지만
저 낯선 하늘 구름조각말고는
아무도 당신을 쳐다보지 않습니다
이렇게 사는 것이 아닌데
허리 펴고 일을 해보려 해도
먹던 밥 치우는 것말고는 없어
어디 나가 걸어보려 해도
깨끗한 낭하 아래론 까마득한 낭떠러지
말 붙일 사람도 걸어볼 사람도 아예 없는
격절의 숨막힌 공간
철컥거리다간 꽝 하고 닫히는 철문 소리
어머니 차라리 창문을 닫으세요
그리고 눈을 감고 당신이 지나쳐온 수많은 자죽

Mother

Mother!
When I see you living so very cautiously
at the top of this so very high apartment block
I think sad thoughts. Is it already three years since you insisted,
up in Pongch'on-dong,
that you would rather die than come and live here?
In the rattling elevator loaded with people
you still get panicky
but once your son and his wife have rushed off to work,
your day's only occupation is to take your grand-daughter
to kindergarten, holding her by the wrist.
Then once the housemaid has cleaned and washed up and left,
once the yogurt delivery woman has shouted and left,
and the woman who cleans the stairs has briskly swept and left,
you open the window and inhale,
high up in flat 7 on the 14th floor, silent as the grave,
but apart from the unfamiliar scraps of cloud in the sky
there's no one looking at you.
This is no way to live but
though you stretch your back and long for work
there's nothing to do except clear away after you've eaten
and supposing you decide to go out for a walk
at the foot of the precipice that borders the spotless corridor
there's no one to speak to, no one to talk to,
just a suffocating void of isolation.
A rattle then a slam as the front door closes:
"For goodness sake, Mother, shut the window!"
Then close your eyes and remember the many traces,

그 갈림길마다 흘린 피눈물들을 기억하세요
없는 집 농사꾼의 맏딸로 태어나
광주 종방의 방직여공이 되었던 게
추운 열여덟 살 겨울이었지요?
이 틀 저 틀로 옮겨 다니며 먼지구덕에서 전쟁물자를 짜다
해방이 되어 돌아와 보니
시집이라 보내준 것이 마름집 병신아들
그 길로 내차고 타향을 떠돌다
손 귀한 어느 양반집 후살이로 들어가
다 잃고 서른이 되어서야 저를 낳았다지요
인공 때는 밤짐을 이고 끌려갔다
하마터면 영 돌아오지 못했을 어머니
죽창으로 당하고 양총으로 당한 것이
어디 한두번인가요
국군이 들어오면 국군에게 밥해주고
밤사람이 들어오면 밤사람에게 밥해주고
이리 뺏기고 저리 뜯기고
쑥국새 울음 들으며 송피를 벗겨
저를 키우셨다지요
모진 세월도 가고
들판에 벼이삭이 자라오르면 처녀적 공장노래 흥얼거리며
이 논 저 논에 파묻혀 초벌 만벌 상일꾼처럼 일하다 끙
달을 이고 돌아오셨지요
비가 오면 덕석걷이, 타작 때면 홀태앗이
누에철엔 뽕걷이, 풀짐철엔 먼 산 가기
여름 내내 삼삼기, 겨우내내 무명잣기
씨 뿌릴 땐 망태메기, 땅 고를 땐 가래잡기
억세고 거칠다고 어버지에게 야단도 많이 맞았지만
머슴들 속에 서면 머슴
밭고랑에 엎드리면 여름 흙내음 물씬 나던
아 좋았던 어머니
그 너른 들 다 팔고 고향을 아주 떠나올 땐

226

the blood and tears shed at every crossing.
Born the eldest girl in a destitute farming family
you went to work in that textile mill in Kwangju
during the bitter winter you turned eighteen, didn't you?
Moving among machines in clouds of dust,
you spun war supplies. With liberation, you went back home
and were married off to the steward's crippled son
so off you went, traveled about, married again, a classy fellow
eager to have kids, lost everything, had me at over thirty.
When the Reds from the North had their way, you were forced
to be a night carrier, as nearly as not failed to come home at all,
so many times you had to face spears and guns.
When the South's army came you cooked for them,
when the other side came you cooked for them.
Robbed by the ones, fleeced by the others,
you stripped off pine needles to the songs of night birds
and brought me up.
Hard times passed too.
When rice sprouted in the plains you'd hum youthful songs
from the factory floor, dig fields, do all kinds of work
like a manual laborer, coming home with the moon high above.
Taking in the coverings of the oxen if it rained,
at threshing time stripping the stalks,
at silkworm time, gathering mulberry leaves,
climbing distant hills at hay-making time,
plaiting flax all summer long,
weaving cotton all winter long,
carrying mesh bags at seed-time,
plowing at earth-leveling time,
Dad used to scold you for being so tough and rough
but really you were just like one of the farmhands.
Mother, I used to be so fond of you,

몇번씩이나 뒤돌아보며 눈물 훔치시며
나 죽으면 저 일하던 진새미밭가에 묻어 달라고 다짐다짐 하시더니
오늘은 이 도시 고층아파트의 꼭대기가
당신을 새처럼 가둘 줄이야 어찌 아셨겠습니까
엘리베이터가 무겁게 열리고 닫히고
어두운 복도 끝에 아들의 구둣발 소리가 들리면
오늘도 구석방 조그만 창을 닫고
조심조심 참았던 숨을 몰아 내쉬는
흰 머리 파뿌리 같은 늙으신 어머니

squatting among the furrows smelling the sweet summer earth.
After you'd sold all those fields, as we left the village for good,
you looked back, wiping tears away, saying, "When I die,
bury me at the side of a field I used to work in."
How could you imagine you'd end cooped up here like a bird
in a cage at the top of this city apartment block?
The elevator doors ponderously open and shut,
your son's footsteps echo at the far end of the dark corridor.
Today again you close your little room's tiny window,
breathing out the breath you had been so carefully holding,
aged mother, with white hair just like the roots of a leek.

서울행

여수발 서울행 밤 열한시 반 비둘기호
말이 좋아 비둘기호 삼등열차
아수라장 같은 통로 바닥에서 고개를 들며
젊은 여인이 내게 물었다
명일동이 워디다요?
등에는 갓난아기 잠들어 있고
바닥에 깐 담요엔
예닐곱 살짜리 사내아이
상기된 표정으로 앉아 있다
야덜 아부지 찾아가는 길이어요
일년 전 실농하고 집을 나갔는디
명일동 워디서 보았다는 사람이 있어.
나는 안다 명일동
대낮에도 광산촌같이 컴컴하던 동네
스피커가 칵칵 악을 쓰고
술 취한 사내들이 큰댓자로 눕고
저녁이 오면 낮은 처마마다
젊은 아낙들의 짧은 비명이 새어나오는 곳
햇볕에 검게 탄, 향기로운 밭이슬이 흐르는
저 여인의 목에도 곧 핏발이 서리라
집 앞 똘물에 빨아 신긴
아이의 새하얀 고무신에도
곧 검은 석탄가루가 묻으리라
그러나 나는 또 안다
그녀가 모든 희망을 걸고 찾아가는 명일동은
이제 서울에 없다는 것을.
엿장수 고물장수 막일꾼들의 거리는 치워지고
바라크 대신 들어선 그린맨션 단지에선

230

In the Train for Seoul

The eleven thirty night train, Pigeon class, from Yosu to Seoul.
The name's nice, Pigeon class, the third class train.
Looking up from the floor of the jam-packed aisle,
a young woman asked me:
"Where can I find Myongil-dong?"
She had a newly-born infant strapped to her back
and on the blanket spread on the floor a boy aged five or six
was sitting with a flushed expression.
"I'm off to find these kids' dad.
He missed last year's farming season, so he left home.
Someone told me they'd seen him in Myongil-dong."
I know that place, Seoul's Myongil-dong;
it used to be as dark as a mining village even at midday,
with public address speakers bawling full blast,
drunks lying sprawled full length,
a place where, when night came,
from beneath each low roof
young women's short cries of pain used to emerge.
On that woman's throat too, burned dark by the sun,
where sweet dew from the fields used to flow,
the veins will soon stand out from shouting.
The kid's clean white rubber shoes, washed in the pure stream
in front of their house, will soon be filthy with coal-dust.
But I know something more: the Myongil-dong
that she is pinning all her hopes on finding no longer exists.
The alleys that used to be full of scrap-merchants, pawn-shops,
day-laborers, are all demolished and gone.
In the grounds of Green Mansions that's replaced the old huts

깨끗한 아이들이 재잘거리며
푸른 잔디 위를 질주하고 있음을.
여수발 서울행 밤 열한시 반 비둘기호
보따리를 풀어 삶은 계란을 내게 권하며
젊은 여인이 불안스레 거듭 물었다
명일동이 워디다요?

spotless children are prattling away
as they go scampering across green lawns.
The eleven thirty night train, third class, from Yosu to Seoul.
The young woman opens her bundle, offers me a boiled egg,
and keeps asking me anxiously:
"Where can I find Myongil-dong?"

잔설을 보며

잔설은 녹고 있다
녹지 않았다
어젯밤 우리가 못다 꾼 꿈처럼
희끗희끗 빛나고 있다
늦은 저녁녘
고속터미널 뒷길이나 한 처녀가 자살한
팔레스 호텔 옆을 지나며
소나무 밑둥치를 발목 깊이 덮고 있는
잔설을 보면
아, 나는 그 뿌리로 내려가
모든 추운 것들을 감싸는
불씨가 되고 싶다
아니, 어디에 닿아도 녹지 않고
스미지 않는, 저 돌멩이 곁 빛나는
차디찬 사랑이 되고 싶다

Traces of Snow

The snow is melting.
But it has not melted yet.
It lies gleaming, spotted with gray,
like the dreams we failed to dream last night.
I glimpse traces of snow
still covering the foot of a pine tree
as I pass late at night
down an alley behind the bus terminal, or pass
Palace Hotel where a girl killed herself.
Oh, I want to turn into a fire
and delve deep to the roots
to protect everything cold.
I want to turn into an icy love
sparkling beside those piles of stones,
refusing to melt or ooze
even if something touches it.

삼십년

깊은 산 외로운 골짜기에
버려진 무덤 하나
풍우에 시달리고 세월에 깎여
작은 돌기만 남은
벌거숭이 무덤
6·25 때 총 맞아 동료를 놓친
한 이름없는 북녘 병사의 것일까
돌아오지 않는 아들을 찾아 헤매다 쓰러진
어느 남녘 어머니의 무덤일까
아무도 다니지 않는 적막 산길에 엎드려
해마다 봄이 오면 무덤 가에 화사한 아기진달래를 피워
건너서 갈 수 없는 찬 벼랑을 불태운다
이편 저편 갈라선 온 민둥산을 불태운다

Thirty Years After

One abandoned grave
stands in a lonely valley high in the hills,
storm-ravaged, time-worn,
nothing left but a little mound of earth.
Perhaps this naked grave
covers a nameless soldier from the north
shot in the wars and left here by his comrades?
Or perhaps it's the tomb of some southern mother
who died wandering in search of a son not come home?
Along the lonely unfrequented path
each spring wild azaleas bloom bright, squat beside the grave,
setting ablaze the cliff beyond, that none can pass,
setting ablaze the barren hillsides rising on either side.

밤

밤은 먼 들의 바람을 몰고 와
십오층 빌딩의 옥상에 부려놓는다
거세게 부딪는 바람소리를 들으면
나는 빈 들로 나아가
한 마리 성난 사랑이 되고 싶다
그러나 밤은 가슴에 더욱 큰 바람을 안고 와
다시 한번 난간을 들이받고
피 흘리며 들판을 헤매다가
새벽녘 가장 강력한 폭풍이되어
그 속에서 무너지지 않는
빛나는 눈동자를 태어나게 한다

Night

Night drives the wind from distant fields,
dumping it on top of a fifteen-story building.
When I hear the wind gusting fiercely,
I long to get out into the fields
and turn into a beast brimming with furious love.
But night comes bringing an even stronger wind
that strikes again against the railings,
wanders off bleeding across the fields,
then at dawn turns into a powerful gale,
giving birth to blazing eyes
that refuse to yield before it.

새

새들은 날아오른다
겨울 추운 북풍 속으로
빠알간 부리를 빛내며
온몸으로 새들은 날아오른다
핏빛 연기 잠든 마을에 더 이상의
큰 슬픔이 없을 때까지
지상에 붙박힌 그들의 영혼을 차며
저 광막한 하늘 위로
노여움 속으로

Birds

Birds go flying up
in winter's bitter wind;
red beaks gleaming,
body and soul, the birds go flying up
until there is no great grief left in the village
where blood-tinged smoke lies sleeping;
spurning their souls too firmly fixed to the ground,
they rise above the far-reaching sky,
up into anger.

공사장 끝에

"지금 부셔버릴까"
"안돼, 오늘밤은 자게 하고 내일 아침에……"
"안돼, 오늘밤은 오늘밤은이 벌써 며칠째야? 소장이 알면……"
"그래도 안돼……"
두런두런 인부들 목소리 꿈결처럼 섞이어 들려오는
루핑집 안 단칸 벽에 기대어 그 여자
작은 발이 삐져나온 어린것들을
불빛인 듯 덮어주고는
가만히 일어나 앉아
칠흑처럼 깜깜한 밖을 내다본다

At the Far End of a Building Site

"Suppose we chuck them out now?"
"No; let them sleep there tonight. Tomorrow morning . . . "
"We can't; all the time 'just for tonight'. If the boss knew . . . "
"Still, we can't . . . "
The laborers' murmurs, confused as in a dream,
    reach the woman
leaning against the thin wall of the corrugated shack;
like fire she covers her babies as they lie
with their little feet sticking out,
rises silently and sits there,
staring into the pitch black night outside.

저녁에

상심한 자의 마음 위에
굽은 어깨 위에
스치며 별이 뜬다
그러면 땅을 뚫고 나온 벌레 한 마리
어디로 가고 있다

In the Evening

Close above the heart of one who grieves,
close above those hunched shoulders,
a star emerges.
Then a single insect emerges from the ground
and hastens on its way.

며눌에게

강물이 풀리면 온다
노들잇벌 갱변으로 온다
다북쑥 피면 나가 보거라
울 너머 송화꽃 펄펄 날리면
애기들 손목 잡고 나가 보거라
수렁내에 젖어서 애비는 온다
소 같은 눈 부릅뜨고 시퍼렇게 온다
뒷모텡이 사립짝에서 보리방아 찧다
가마니 속에 피아골로 끌려간 자식
내 인제 꽃상여에 덮여
꼬부랑탕 저 고개 넘어가버리면
언제나 만나볼꼬 그립운 자식
동구앞 돌아보며 돌아보며 설한풍 속에 먼저 간다고 일러주거라
저승가 개울 가에서 혹 마주치면
거기 지팽이 짚고 먼 산 바래는 누더기 할미가
이 에미라고 전해주거라
깨꽃이 필 때면 나가 보거라
씀부기 울음 문풍지에 바르르 쑥빛으로 물들면
노들잇벌 갱변으로 나가 보거라
강물이 풀리면 온다고 했다
노들잇벌 갱변으로 온다고 했다

To a Daughter-in-law

When the river abates, he will come.
Along the far river bank, he will come.
When the mugwort blooms, go out and look.
When pine pollen drifts beyond the fence,
take the children by the hand, go out and look.
Your Dad is coming, soaked in the marsh.
Deadly pale, cow-like eyes glaring, your Dad is coming.
As he pounded barley by the brushwood back gate,
my son was taken, carried away in a rice bag to Piakol.
Once I am borne off in the flowered bier
zigzagging up over the hill,
when shall we meet again, darling boy?
Tell him I am going first in the icy wind,
gazing back, gazing back at the village entrance.
And if we happen to meet by some riverside in the other world
explain that the tattered old woman carrying a stick
gazing up toward distant hills
is his mother.
When sesame flowers bloom, go out and look.
When the weather stripping rustles pale as marsh hens coo,
go out and look along the far river bank
He said he would come when the river abates.
He said he would come along the far river bank.

고개

앞산길 첩첩 뒷산길 첩첩
돌아보면 정든 봉 첩첩
아재야 아재아 정갭이 아재야
지게목 떨어진다 한가락 뽑아라
네 소리 아니고는 못 넘어가겠다
기러기떼 돌아 넘는 천황재 아홉 굽이
내 오늘 너를 묶어 이 고개 넘는다만
언제나 벗어나리,
가도 가도 서러운 머슴살이 우리 신세
청포꽃 되어 너는 언덕 아래 살짝 필래
파랑새 되어 푸른 하늘 훨훨 날래
한 주인을 벗어나면 또 다른 주인
한 세월 섬기고 나면 더 검은 세월
못 살아가겠다고 못 참겠다고 너도 울고 나도 울고
쩌렁쩌렁 울었지만
오늘은 찬 바람에 봉두난발 날리며
말없이 너도 넘고 나도 넘는다
묏새들 저러이 울어 예
차마 발 떨어지지 않는 느티목 고개,
묶인 너 부여안고 한번 넘으면 그만인 아, 죽살잇 고개를

The Hill

Endless hill paths ahead, endless hill paths behind,
all around endless peaks so dear.
Ajeya ajeya chonggebi ajeya: sing something, do,
for the frame on my back is wearing me out.
Without your song, I'll never get to the top.
Today I climb this hill with you bound to me,
wild geese soar over the nine bends of Ch'onhwang Peak
but when shall we get past?
On and on we go, grim field work we laborers' burden but
will you be a blue flower bright at the foot of the hill,
a bluebird flying light in the blue sky above?
Leaving one master, another master awaits
serving for one season, another dark season awaits:
I can't go on, I can't take any more, you wept, I wept,
we wept aloud
yet today, unkempt hair ruffled by the icy wind,
without a word, you climb on, I climb on.
All the birds singing sadly, ah,
my feet will not move on up Nutimok Hill,
cherishing you, holding you bound to me,
once over it's over, up Life and Death Hill . . .

수평선

밤새도록 파도는 몸부림치면서 일어서면서 신음하면서
아침이 오면
거기 달랑
젊은 섬 하나를 낳는다
뜨거운 은빛 등을 보이며 떠올랐다 난바다에 떨어지는
아침 수평선의 서늘함이여

Horizon

All night long the waves writhe, rise, moan
then, when morning comes,
they give birth to one young island
simply there,
coolness of the morning horizon
showing its hot silver back rising and falling in the open sea

편지

낙엽의 계절입니다
부리 긴 새들의 철도 끝났습니다
지난 여름 우리는 너무 오래 싸웠습니다
남녘의 들판은 아우가 흘린 피로 검붉었으며
핵탄두가 겨눈 북녘 하늘은
또 매섭게 푸르렀습니다
형제여 그러나 이 계절의 끝에
더욱 큰 시련의 계절이 닥쳐옵니다
눈보라 칼바람 속에서 남쪽의 어미가 아비를 떠나보내고
얼어붙은 국경의 강을 건너
북의 아들이 돌아올 것입니다
그리고 기나긴 사상의 전쟁이 끝나고
우리 모두가 죽고
두꺼웠던 얼음이 녹는 강언덕 위로
아직 태어나지 않은 아이들의
쩌렁쩌렁한 새 봄이 밝아올 것입니다

A Letter

This is the season of fallen leaves,
the season of long-beaked birds is over too.
Last summer we fought for far too long.
The fields in the south grew dark red with brothers' blood
while skies in the north, targeted by nuclear warheads,
grew more fiercely blue.
But brother dear, at the end of this season
a season of even greater ordeals is approaching.
In biting blizzards the mothers of the south see the fathers off
and beyond the frozen border river
the sons of the north will return again.
Then the long war between ideologies will end,
we will all die
and over the river hills where the thick ice is melting
a new spring will dawn with resonant cries,
the spring of children yet unborn.

역사에 대하여

그때 산야에서 싸운 사람들은
진실을 남기지 않았다
남길 시간조차 없었다
다만 산천의 어느 타오르는 등성이에
그들의 뼈를 눕혔다
수십년 후
피아골行 굴착공사장의 검은 흙 아래 드러난
저 수많은 주검들의 아우성과
대낮 인부들 어깨 사이로
이제 막 무릎을 털고 일어서는
늙은 산의 먹물 같은 외로움

About History

The people who fought over moor and mountain
left no truth behind.
They had not even time to leave it.
Their bones simply lay scattered
on the burning ridges of some mountain view.
Decades later what remains?
The shouts of those countless corpses
buried beneath the black earth where they're building
the road up Piakol Valley
and between the daytime workers' shoulders
as they rise to their feet with trembling knees
the old mountain's loneliness like deep black ink.

* *Piakol Valley is in Chiri-san (Chiri Mountain). It was the scene of violent confrontations between communist partisans and anti-communist forces.*

형제들을 위하여

1897년생인 우리 아버지가 이 세상에 와서
뻑적지근하게 이룬 것이 있다면
그것은 자식을 열이나 낳았다는 것이다
한 배에서가 아니고 두 배에서지만
그리고 다 살리진 못하고 그 중에 여섯이나
당신 손으로 뒷산 애장터에 묻어야 했지만
오늘밤 아파트 창문을 활짝 열어놓고
일생 농군 학생부군(學生府君)께 술 한잔 올리니
어려서 죽은 우리 형제들이 천릿길을 달려와
애기두루마기 차림으로
이 방 저 방에 TV 앞에 시집간 누이들 틈서리에
듬성듬성 앉아 있는 것 같으이다
삼식(三植)이 형님 기식(寄植)이 형님 일학년짜리
명식(明植)이 형 해방둥이 명자(明子) 누나
나보다 두 살 위 후식(厚植)이 형 이름도 없이 가물거리는 내 아랫동생
초헌 아헌 종헌이 끝나고 다 함께 음복하고
검은 재와 함께 새벽별 스러질 때까지
내 핏속에 애기들의 여린 숨결 속에 살아
어서 가자고 칭얼대는 어린 동생을 달래가며
밤새도록 도란도란 이야기하고 있는 것 같으이다

For my Brothers

If there was one splendid thing achieved by our father,
who came into this world in 1897,
it was the fact of having ten kids.
Not all from one womb, it's true, but from two,
and they didn't all survive, some six of them
he had to bury with his own hands in the burial ground
up on the hill behind the house
but tonight, opening the apartment windows wide,
I offer a glass of wine to my dead father's soul;
he was a peasant all his life.
Then those brothers of mine who died in childhood come
hurrying from far away, in old-fashioned children's clothes,
and seem to be sitting here and there in this room and that
in front of the TV among their now married sisters.
My elder brothers Sam-sik and Ki-sik, with Myong-sik
who died in his first year at school, as well as Myong-ja,
my sister born in '45, the Year of Liberation,
my brother Hu-sik, two years above me, and the youngest one,
I've forgotten his name.
Candles, incense, wine offered, then all drink together,
after burning the paper soul-tablets,
until the morning star fades,
alive in my blood and the little ones' breath,
comforting my youngest brother as he whimpers to be off
I seem to spend all night long in whispered yarns.

눈 내리는 밤에

이런 밤엔 먼 산에서 승냥이들이 뛴다
토끼들도 먹이를 찾아
놀란 눈을 두리번거리며
어느 새 마을 길까지 내려와 있다

아, 한 차례 새벽 바람이 휩쓸고 가버리는
토끼네 식구들의 뜨겁고도 진지한 발자국

One Snowy Evening

On a night like this, wolves are leaping in distant hills.
Hares hunting for food
glance about with fearful eyes
as they come down unawares into the village streets.

Aha, the warm sober tracks of a family of hares,
swept away in a flash by a dawn gust of wind.

곶에서

하늘의 별처럼 많은 시인
바다의 모래처럼 많은 사람
그러나 그 중에도 밤이 깊을수록 홀로 뚜렷이 빛을 머금은 별 있고
해풍 거셀수록 숨결 가득 안으로 닦이는 모래 있었네
바람 자고 하늘 맑은 날 나는 보았네
그 별 하나 꽃처럼 터지기 위하여
수많은 작은 별들의 피흘림 있었고
그 모래 하나 크나큰 침묵으로 뭍에 오르기 위해
수많은 다른 파도들의 숨가쁜 침잠이 있었음을
하늘의 별처럼 맑고 푸른 빛
바다의 모래처럼 늙고 잔잔한 바람

On a Cape

Poets are as numerous as the stars in the sky.
People are as numerous as the sand in the sea.
Yet as night grew dark one star alone was shedding light.
As the sea breeze roughened, inhaling deeply
one grain of sand was being polished by it.
One day when the wind slept and the sky was clear,
I understood: for that one star to shine like a flower,
the blood of a host of little stars was shed.
For that one grain of sand to come to land in enormous silence,
a host of other waves lay gasping becalmed.
Hue bright and blue as a star in the sky.
Wind old and still as the sand in the sea.

새

아침 산길의 눈밭 위에는 머리가 상한 참새 두 마리가 서로의
날갯죽지에 핏빛 새근대는 부리를 묻은 채 잠들어 있었습니다

이 도시에 새들의 영혼까지도 앗아가 버리는
무서운 계엄군이 진입하던 날

Birds

On a patch of snow beside the mountain path this morning,
two sparrows lay with bleeding heads, asleep with their
gasping blood-red beaks buried under each other's wings.

Today dreaded martial law troops occupied the city,
driving even the little birds out of their minds.

골짜기

골짜기에 비가 내리면
어디서 칭얼거리는 소리가 들립니다

키 큰 상수리나무 잎사귀가 그 소리를 듣고는 발밑의 애기무덤을 토닥토닥 달래는 소리가 들려옵니다. "아가 아가 우지 마라. 너 울음 울면 산 내려간 네 어머니 발 떨어지지 않는다. 비가 오면 가려주마, 눈 내리면 덮어 주마. 명년 삼월 삼짇날 애기제비들 돌아오고 네 무덤에 파릇파릇 새 잔디 돋을 때까지 이 아저씨 너를 지켜주마. 아가 아가 우지 마라. 잠든 너를 내려놓고 집에 간 네 어머니 애간장 녹는다."

골짜기에 비가 내리면
어디서 혹 느껴우는 소리가 들려옵니다
그리고 온 산이 품을 모아 그 소리를 깊이 껴안는 소리가 들립니다

264

A Valley

In the valley, as the rain fell
a sound of whimpering could be heard.

The leaves of a towering oak tree noticed it and a rapping sound could be heard consoling the baby that lay in a grave at its feet: "Baby, baby, don't cry. Your mother's gone down the mountain and if you cry, her feet cannot move. If it rains, I'll shelter you, if it snows I'll cover you. Until the third day of the third month next year when the little swallows return and fresh green grass sprouts upon your grave, I'll care for you. Baby, baby, don't cry. Your mother laid you here and went back down; now her heart is shattered."

In the valley, as the rain falls
a sound of sobbing can be heard.
Then the whole mountain can be heard gathering it up and deeply hugging that sound to its heart.

노래

사랑한다는 사랑한다는 그 말 한마디 전해드리기 위해
이 강에 섰건만
바람 이리 불고 강물 저리 붉어
못 건너가겠네 못 가겠네

잊어버리라 잊어버리라던 그 말 한마디 돌려드리기 위해
이 산마루에 섰건만
천둥 이리 우짖고 비바람 속 낭 저리 깊어
못 다가가겠네 못 가겠네

낭이라면 아득한 낭에 핀 한떨기 꽃처럼,
강이라면 숨막히는 바위 속, 거센 물살을 거슬러오르는
은빛 찰나의 물고기처럼

A Song

I love you, I love you: to speak those words
I came out and stood on this river bank
but the breezes blow here, the waters glow there,
I cannot go over, I cannot go.

Forget me, forget, you said: to return those words
I came and stood on this mountain ridge
but thunder rolls here, storm-girded cliffs tower there,
I cannot go closer, I cannot go.

If it's a cliff, like flowers blooming on a forbidding cliff;
if it's a river, I'll be like a silver fish glimpsed fighting its way
upstream against a fierce current among choking rocks.

그대

그대는 늘 밝고 먼 미소 가운데 있어
둥그러운 빛을 내게 주시니
공중을 깊이 나는 새들도 그 빛을 오래 끌어당기며
고요의 기쁨 날개 떨도다

봄

사형장 높은 담벽 위에도 봄이 왔습니다
그리하여 바람 불고 햇빛 밝은 날
작년에 쌓인 눈 속에서
예쁜 강아지풀을 하늘하늘 피웠습니다

You

You are always surrounded with far-reaching bright smiles,
you bestow on me a ring of light;
even the birds flying high in the air tug long at that light
as they flap their wings in silent joy.

Springtime

Spring also came over the high walls of the execution ground
until one day as the breezes blew and the sun shone bright
in the midst of last year's drifted snow
pretty foxtails blossomed dancing lightly.

저 산을 보면

저 산을 보면 내 마음에 불이 붙는다
겨우내 옥창 사이로 바라보았던
흰뼈만으로 간신히 자기를 지키던 산
그러나 오늘은 옆구리에 가득 푸르른 새끼봉들을 안고
그 넓은 맨가슴으로 봄눈을 맞는다 봄눈을 맞는다

내관 (內觀)

나를 죽여
내 안의 나를 심화, 확장하는 일
나를 죽여
내 안의 내 마른 나뭇가지에 동백 두어 송이
        후끈하게 피워올리는 일
나를 죽여
싸락눈 때리는 날
내 마음의 빈 대숲에 푸른 칼날 수천 개를 일렁이게 하는 일
낮은 바람에도 저를 향해 부드럽게 구부러지게 하는 일

When I See That Hill

When I see that hill, my heart catches fire.
The hill that all winter long I used to glimpse
through the prison windows
barely surviving with its pale white ribs
today is hugging to itself a host of baby peaks,
its vast bare breast exposed to springtime snow,
exposed to springtime snow.

Contemplation

Kill me
all that deepens and widens the me within me
kill me
all that brings camellias budding, flowering crimson
on the dry branches within me
kill me
on a day of hail showers
all that brings thousands of steely knife-blades swaying
     in my heart's empty bamboo grove,
that makes them gently incline toward me
     in the lightest breeze.

저물녘

저물녘 먼 하늘에 띠를 두르고 선
남빛 산의 완강한 부드러움이여
가서 그 어깨 뒤로 서고 싶다

강추위

바람은 몽고바람아 쌩쌩 몰아쳐 와라
이 바람 속에는 중강진 혜산진을 지키는
수비대 병사들의 뜨거운 뺨 기운도 깃들어 있다

Sunset

The stubborn gentleness of the indigo hill
that rears, tightly belted, in the distant sunset sky!
How I long to stand behind its shoulder.

Dry Cold

Come now, winds, sharp Mongolian winds.
In this wind, the warm cheeks of the sentries guarding
the camps of Chungkang and Hyesan are muffled tight.

연봉(連峰)

 산천은 결코 의구하지만은 않다는, 어느 지리산 빨치산 수기의
'머리말'을 읽다가 가슴이 뭉클했습니다. 그렇습니다. 사람의
삶이 그러한 것처럼 산의 생명 또한 끝없는 변화 속에 있습니다.
그때 그 찢긴 산등성이에서 불거져나온 피투성이 아이가 자라
마흔살의 장년이 되었듯 당신의 젊은 전사들과 함께 피 토하며
쓰러졌던 비운의 산들도 세월의 흐름 속에 조금씩 새살 돋아
어느 산은 새로 아기 산이 되고 어느 산은 끝내 한쪽 어깨를 못
쓰기도 하면서 가을볕에 저렇게 살아 젊고 늙은 얼굴도
눈부십니다.

노래

 깊은 산 골짜기에 막 얼어붙은 폭포의 숨결
 내년 봄이 올 때까지 거기 있어라
 다른 입김이 와서 그대를 녹여줄 때까지

Mountain Peaks

"Mountains and rivers do not always stay unchanged."

Reading those words in the preface to the journal of a Chiri-san partisan, I found myself choked with emotion. I felt that it was so true. The mountain's life, just like our human life, is plunged in endless change. Just as the child that came gore-covered into the world up on that jagged ridge has by now grown into a man in his forties, so with the ongoing flow of time the hills too, those hills that fell when your brave young warriors fell, coughing blood, have gradually grown new layers of skin; some hills have become new baby hills, and some have finally lost the use of one shoulder; they rise now dazzling in the autumn light, alive with young and old faces.

A Song

Stay where you are until next spring comes,
breath of cascades frozen solid now in high ravines,
until another breath comes and makes you melt.

미카 16

자라서 한번도 그곳에 닿은 적 없는데도
마음이 먼저 달려가 환한 전깃불 켜고 기다리는 곳 있지?
내게 그곳은 전라선 외가닥 철로의 작은 점 주생, 옹정, 금지역

이른 저녁 무렵이었을까, 아니면 환한 대낮이었을까
오수, 서도, 남원의 협곡을 빠져나온 열차가 모처럼 너른 벌을 만나
들까불며 빽빽 경쾌한 기적을 울리고 검은 석탄 연기를 내뿜으면
일대의 정적이 생기로 뒤바뀌는 극적인 순간을 나는 보았다
아무 일도 없었던 듯 엎드려 있던 들판이
갑자기 똥그란 눈을 뜨고 달려나오고
저녁 연기 오르는 대숲 마을을 향해
느릿느릿 소걸음을 떼어가던 소년의 발이 재게 빨라지고
나락 사이로 반쯤 고개를 든 밀짚모자 농부의 얼굴이
하늘 아래 가장 천연한 웃음으로 빛나던 것을
나 이제껏 한번도 그곳에 내린 적 없지만
전라북도 남원역 아래 측백나무 울타리
미카 16 완행열차가 하늘을 향해 기쁜 목을 잠시 들었다 가는
주생역이나 옹정, 혹은 가는귀 아주 작게 먹은 낮은 금지역

Mica 16

Although we have never been back since growing up, surely
we all have places the heart hurries towards,
switching on the light and waiting? For me, it's some tiny stops
on the single-track Cholla railway: Chuseng, Ongjong, Kumji.

Was it in the early evening? Or in broad daylight?
Trains from Osu, Sodo, Namwon, emerging from the ravine,
finally encountering open countryside, rocking lightly,
they whistled brightly, puffed out pitch black coal smoke,
and I experienced dramatic moments as the usual stillness
was transformed into bustling motion.
The fields, that had been prostrate as if with nothing to do,
suddenly opened wide eyes and came dashing up, the steps
of the lads that had gone traipsing off at a snail's pace
towards woodland villages veiled in evening smoke
took on new speed, straw-hatted farmers' faces
half sunk between their shoulders
lit up with the most natural smile in the world,
I have never once got down
past Namwon station in North Cholla, at Chuseng station, or
Ongjong, or little Kumji station, just slightly deaf,
with their thuja tree fences,
as the train Mica 16 rests its cheerful head a moment.

봄

충남 연기군 남면 상공을
아기 갈매기 네 마리가 눈부신 흰 깃을 펄럭이며
일직선으로 난다
아아, 첫 비상이다

무늬

나뭇잎들이 포도 위에 다소곳이 내린다
저 잎새 그늘을 따라 가겠다는 사람이 옛날에 있었다

In Springtime

In South Ch'unchong's Yongi county, in the skies of Nam-myon,
four young gulls flap dazzling white wings
as they fly in a straight line.
Their very first flight!

Pattern

Leaves flutter meekly to the sidewalk.
Once there was someone who promised
to follow those leaves' shadows.

신새벽

한밤중에 깨어 일어나
내가 갑자기 착한 소가 될 때가 있다

이때가 가장 정다운 때!
넓은 귀를 늘어뜨리고
내가 더 깊숙한 나로 태어날 때!

우주의 저 까마득한 밑바닥에서
쨍그랑 하고 돌멩이 하나 깨어지는 소리 들린다

향기로운 땅 새벽이 가차이 열리는 것은 이때부터
그리운 그리운 파도가 먼 해안선을 초록 띠로 물들이는 것도 이때부터

A New Dawn

There are moments when I wake and get up in the night,
suddenly turned into an obedient cow.

Those are the truest moments of all!
Moments when I am reborn as a deeper version of myself
with big dangling ears.

From the remotest depths of the cosmos
rings the crash of a rock being smashed.

Now dawn gently opens over the fragrant land
and the waves I long for, long for,
tint the distant shoreline with a sash of green

김수영조(金洙暎調)로

시를 읽자
부지런히 읽자
네 영혼에 때가 끼기 전에
시도 쓰자
부지런히 쓰자
마른 영혼이 바람에 불려가지 않게
묵직한 놈으로
시의 길은 처음 가는 길
아무도 가지 않은 길을
처음으로 처음으로 가는 길

Poem ... à la Kim Su-Young

Let's read poetry
let's keep reading poetry
and before your soul gets dirty
let's write poetry
let's keep writing poetry
as a weighty kind of fellow
to prevent your dry soul being blown away by the wind
poetry's path is a path taken for the first time ever
a path no one has ever taken before
a path taken for the very first very first time.

조금 후

까우까우
강 건너 저쪽에서 누가 알은체한다
꺼우꺼우
강 건너 이쪽에서 내가 알은체한다

까우까우 꺼우꺼우…
까우까우 끄우끄우…
문득, 하늘엔 물빛 깃 치는 소리
그대와 나 사이에 서광 있으라

After a While

Caw caw
From across the river, someone is calling.
Cao cao
From this side of the river, I am calling.

Caw caw, cao cao.
Caw caw, cwo cwo.
Suddenly comes a sound of azure wings beating in the sky.
I wish day would dawn between you and me.

숲에 가면

숲에 가면 좋은 일이 있을 듯하다
덤불 속에 아직 온기 남은 작은 멧새알 하나,
바위 모서리를 뚫고 샘솟는 뜨거운 石間水 한 모금,
숲에 가면 오래 잊은 좋은 일이 있을 듯하다

If We Go to the Woods

If we go to the woods, something good may happen—
a little bunting's egg still warm from a bush,
a draught of spring water trickling warm from a rock—
if we go to the woods something good, long forgotten,
may happen.

마음의 고향 2
— 그 언덕

왜 그곳이 자꾸 안 잊히는지 몰라
가름젱이 사래 긴 우리 밭 그 건너의 논실 이센 밭
가장자리에 키 작은 탱자 울타리가 쳐진.
훗날 나 중학생이 되어
아침마다 콩밭 이슬을 무릎으로 적시며
그곳을 지나다녔지
수수알이 꽝꽝 여무는 가을이었을까
깨꽃이 하얗게 부서지는 햇빛 밝은 여름날이었을까
아랫냇가 굽이치던 물길이 옆구리를 들이받아
벌건 황토가 드러난 그곳
허리 굵은 논실댁과 그의 딸 영자 영숙이 순임이가
밭 사이로 일어섰다 앉았다 하며 커다란 웃음들을 웃고
나 그 아래 냇가에 소 고삐를 풀어놓고
어항을 놓고 있었던가 가재를 쫓고 있었던가
나를 부르는 소리 같기도 하고
쏴르르 쏴르르 무엇이 물살을 헤짓는 소리 같기도 하여
고개를 들면 아, 청청히 푸르던 하늘
갑자기 무섬증이 들어 언덕 위로 달려오르면
들꽃 싸아한 향기 속에 두런두런 논실댁의 목소리와
까르르 까르르 밭 가장자리로 울려퍼지던
영자 영숙이 순임이의 청랑한 웃음 소리
나 그곳에 오래 앉아
푸른 하늘 아래 가을 들이 또랑또랑 익는 냄새며
잔돌에 호미 달그락거리는 소리 들었다
왜 그곳이 자꾸 안 잊히는지 몰라
소를 몰고 돌아오다가
혹은 객지로 나가다가 들어오다가

288

The Heart's Own Home   2
— that hill

I don't know why I cannot forget that spot,
old Nonsil's paddy across from our field
with its boundary hedge of small thorny orange trees.
Later, when I was in middle school, I would pass that spot
wet to the knees with dew from the soy-bean fields.
Was it autumn, when the sorghum seeds ripen?
A bright summer day with sunlight smashing down
pure and white on sesame flowers?
At the spot where the stream lower down
had eroded its banks, exposing the reddish ocher soil,
Nonsil's stout wife and her lovely daughters, Yongja, Yongsuk
and Sunim, were bellowing with laughter as they stood
then squatted between the fields. Beside the stream I untied
the cow's halter; then what? Did I put bait in a bowl for fish?
Chase after crawfish? I heard a sound, a voice calling me,
a *swish-swash* as if something was disturbing the stream.
Looking up, ah, I saw the dazzling blue sky.
Seized with sudden panic, I went rushing up the hillside,
through the pungent fragrance surrounding the flowers,
Nonsil's murmur, the laughter of Yongja, Yongsuk and Sunim
spreading clear beyond the edges of the field.
I sat there for a long time with the smell of autumn fields
ripening bright and right under the blue sky,
listening to the sound of hoes scraping against stones.
I don't know why I cannot forget that spot.
After driving the cow to pasture
or coming back from somewhere, on my return

무엇이 나를 부르는 것 같아
나 오래 그곳에 서 있곤 했다

I used to stand at that spot for hours.
Something seemed to be calling me.

바람

잎새가 살랑인다

어제 내 목덜미를 감싸며 흐느끼던 말 못할 숨결이
오늘 잎새를 저리 뜨겁게 관통했으리

푸른 하늘

잿빛 거위가 긴 목을 곧게 펴고 노란 철갑의 부리를 마구 휘두
르며 운다

하늘엔 살짝 깔린 옅은 흰구름
그 여울을 빠르게 건너는 잠자리의 여린 날개가 있다

Wind

The leaves are trembling.
The indescribable breath that yesterday
wrapped my throat whimpering,
must be most warmly piercing the leaves today.

Blue Sky

A gray gander stretches its long neck straight, shakes its
yellow-coated beak, and calls.

In the sky, are lightly spread white clouds
and the delicate wings of dragonflies fording those rapids.

자본주의

밤 일곱시, 마포주차장에 어둠이 내리면 수백 개의 백열등이 밝고 어디서 놀란 고양이들이 눈을 흡뜨고 낮 동안 굳게 닫혔던 차단기가 오르고 질주의 본능을 이기지 못한 자동차들이 붕붕거리며 썰물처럼 정문을 빠져 나가면, 밤 아홉시. 마포주차장에 정적이 내리면 어디서 공허란 놈이 거대한 하품을 하며 턱을 떨고 일어나 납빛 하늘 밑을 서성거리다 차단기를 발견하고는 갑자기 두 눈에 사나운 짐승의 불을 켜고 질주하다가 견고한 철책에 머리를 박고 나동그라진다. 밤 열두시. 미지근한 바람 부는 마포주차장의 견딜 수 없는 백열등 아래 공허의 흰 피가 붉다.

Capitalism

7pm, at Map'o parking lot as night falls, hundreds of lights
come on, somewhere startled cats open wide eyes, the gate that
was firmly closed all day is raised, as cars unable to control
their instinct for speeding emerge from the main entrance like
an ebbing tide, 9pm, at Map'o parking lot as silence falls,
somewhere Emptiness yawns widely, shakes its jowls, stands
up, goes strolling about beneath the leaden sky then discovers
the gate and suddenly both its eyes blaze with the glare of a
fierce animal, as it goes speeding, slams its head against some
railings and falls sprawling. 12 midnight, beneath the
unbearable lights at Map'o parking lot swept by a tepid wind,
Emptiness's pale blood glows crimson.

어떤 개인 날

지난 여름 장미비에 찢긴 가지에
새봄 들어 간신히 잎을 피워놨더니
올여름 장대비는 그걸 모르고
그 아픈 자릴 또 사정없이 꺽어버리네

귀가

누군가의 구둣발이 지렁이 한 마리를 밟고 지나갔다
그 발은 뚜벅뚜벅 걸어가
그들만의 단란한 식탁에서 환히 웃고 있으리라
지렁이 한 마리가 포도에서 으깨어진 머리를 들어
간신히 집 쪽을 바라보는 동안

A Fine Day

On branches battered by last summer's rains,
leaves struggled to emerge when spring came.
This year's summer rains know nothing of that;
they smash mercilessly at the wounded place again.

Going Home

Someone's boots crushed an earthworm in passing.
Those feet marched on and they
are now laughing cheerfully at the merry family supper table
while the worm lifts its crushed head from the sidewalk
and agonizingly gazes homeward.

새벽에

벌레들이 먼저 일어나
저렇듯 우주의 한쪽을 파랗게 물들이고 있었구나

아슬한 거처

저 보잘것없는 가지 위로 참새 몇 마리가 내려앉자
나무가 휘청하면서 세계의 중심을 새로 잡는다
아람드리 바람이 불어왔다가 불어간다 가지가 흔들린다
참새들의 작은 눈이 바쁘게 움직이고
그 위로 곧 어두운 저녁이 내린다

At Dawn

Why, the insects rose early
and set about coloring one portion of the universe blue!

Perilous Dwelling

A few sparrows perch on an insignificant branch,
at which the tree bends, then rightens the cosmic balance again.
A pillar of wind comes and goes; the branch shakes.
The sparrows' little eyes move busily
as evening darkness drops from above.

새해 달력을 보다

그는 오늘 아침에도 어김없이 출근했으며
어제 아침에도 어김없이 출근했으며
그제 아침에도 어김없이 출근했으며
죽지 않는다면 내일 아침에도 어김없이 출근할 것이며
아 그런데 창 밖에 함박눈이 내린다
쌓인 눈 속에 거위가 온몸을 묻고
목만 내민 채 조용히 좌선중이시다
좁쌀 같은 참새들이 다가와 아는 체를 해도
거구의 경비 아저씨가 다가와 발을 굴러도
눈을 감으신 채 조용히 좌선중이시다

New Year's Calendar

This morning he went to work as he should
and yesterday morning he went to work as he should
and the day before he went to work as he should
and unless he dies, tomorrow morning too
he'll go to work as he should
and meanwhile it's snowing outside.
A goose buries itself in the drifting snow,
until only its head appears, and meditates quietly.
Fussy sparrows come along expecting a greeting,
the big caretaker comes along, stamping his feet;
it continues to sit in meditation, eyes firmly closed.

The Translators

Brother Anthony of Taizé

Brother Anthony was born in 1942 in Truro (U.K.). He studied Medieval and Modern Languages at The Queen's College, Oxford. In 1969, he joined the Community of Taizé (France), came to Korea in May 1980, and was naturalized in 1994 with the Korean name An Sonjae. He is Professor at Sogang University (Seoul), teaching English literature.

In addition to the six books of Korean poetry co-translated with Young-moo Kim listed below, Brother Anthony has published *The Early Lyrics of So Chong Ju (Midang)* and *The Poet*, a novel by Yi Mun-yol (translated with Chung Chong-hwa) as well as three volumes of poems by Ku Sang. *The Poet* was awarded the 1995 Daesan Translation Award.

Young-Moo Kim

Young-Moo Kim was born in 1944 in Paju, near Seoul. After earning his B.A. and M.A. from the English Department of Seoul National University, he received his Ph.D. from the English Department of SUNY at Stony Brook. He has been Professor in the Department of English Language and Literature at Seoul National University since 1981. He is a literary critic and has also published two volumes of his own poems in Korean.

He and Brother Anthony have together translated and published *The Sound of my Waves* and *Beyond Self* by Ko Un, *Back to Heaven* by Ch'on Sang-Pyong, *Faint Shadows of Love* by Kim Kwang-kyu, and *Farmers' Dance* by Shin Kyong-Nim. Their volume of Kim Kwang-Kyu won the Translation Prize in the 1991 Republic of Korea Literary Awards, and the Ch'on Sang-Pyong volume was awarded the 1996 Korean PEN Translation Prize.

CORNELL EAST ASIA SERIES

FORTHCOMING

To order, please contact the Cornell East Asia Series, East Asia Program, Cornell University, 140 Uris Hall, Ithaca, NY 14853-7601, USA; phone (607) 255-6222, fax (607) 255-1388, ceas@cornell.edu, http://www.einaudi.cornell.edu/bookstore/eap

SB/6-01/1.2 M pb/.3M hc